Moved by Love

The story of an ordinary woman who is living an extraordinary life

By Marsha D. Thomas

FOREWORD

This book is for struggling women who are in need of redemption and restoration.
This book is also for women who have overcome and who have won the war.
The battles still come up, but now you are equipped!

This book is first dedicated to God—for His Love, His Care and His Guidance. He calms my spirit and gives me Peace. Next, it is dedicated to my parents.

Both have never been 30 miles outside of their adopted homes. One didn't get out of elementary school, junior high for the other. Yet they inspired eight children to go to college and one to see the world. Next, it is dedicated to my children who have become my greatest teachers, and my grandchildren who are my greatest loves.

Lastly, I dedicate this book to everyone who has come into my life. I am a firm believer that everyone who comes into my life brings me a gift, no exception. Sometimes that gift is buried under a lot of "stuff," but the gift is there nevertheless. Sometimes, it is like peeling an onion to get to the gift. I am sure that people have had to drill down to my core to really understand me and see the gift that I bring also. So today I say thank you for your gift!

I am, because my ancestors were. They were because God is. We must keep moving forward. We must be moved by love!

INTRODUCTION

If I speak in the tongues of men and of angels, but have not love, I am a noisy gong or a clanging cymbal. And if I have prophetic powers, and understand all mysteries and all knowledge, and if I have all faith, so as to remove mountains, but have not love, I am nothing. If I give away all I have, and if I deliver up my body to be burned, but have not love, I gain nothing.

Love is patient and kind; love does not envy or boast; it is not arrogant or rude. It does not insist on its own way; it is not irritable or resentful; it does not rejoice at wrongdoing, but rejoices with the truth. Love bears all things, believes all things, hopes all things, endures all things.

Love never ends. As for prophecies, they will pass away; as for tongues, they will cease; as for knowledge, it will pass away. For we know in part and we prophesy in part, but when the perfect comes, the partial will pass away. When I was a child, I spoke like a child, I thought like a child, I reasoned like a child. When I became a man, I gave up childish ways. For now we see in a mirror dimly, but then face to face. Now I know in part; then I shall know fully, even as I have been fully known.

So now faith, hope, and love abide, these three; but the greatest of these is love.

— I Corinthians 13 (English Standard Version)

Most people are familiar with the above scriptures. And people will tell you this is "agape" love, the purest form of love. People will tell you that it doesn't exist here. They will tell you this is a picture of God's love for us. But what if I told you we could manifest this type of love right here on Earth and in our own lives? But you can't have love without forgiveness that leads to redemption for all.

Anger is like you taking poison and hoping someone else dies. Forgiveness doesn't mean that you forget, but it does say you give up the right to punish someone for the hurt they caused.

Love has healing power! It is redemptive and restorative.

Love is not a noun. It is an action verb.

I charge each one of you reading this to let love roll down like rain. Why not spread Love like a contagious virus? It will require a conscious effort. I didn't say it would be easy. I am just saying that it is worth it!

Let's start a "Love Revolution."

And when you feel like giving up, just remember: "A three-stranded cord is not easily broken."

TABLE OF CONTENTS

Part I: The Early Years

    a. Chapter 1: Mind Body and Spirit
    b. Chapter 2: The Power of 12
    c. Chapter 3: Life Happens
    d. Chapter 4: Descent into Chaos (a diamond is not honed by water but by fire)

Part II: The Middle Years
    a. Chapter 5: The Ascension
    a. Chapter 6: The Call That Would Change My Life
    b. Chapter 7: I Am Drinking From My Saucer
    c. Chapter 8: Getting the Assignment

Part III: Moving into The Present
    a. Chapter 9: Your Future is So Bright, You Need Sunglasses
    b. Chapter 10: African American Proverbs & Home Remedies

CHAPTER 1

Mind, Body and Spirit—Making the Connection

"We are Spiritual creatures just having a human experience."

When I first started attending conferences that were not work related, I happened to sit in on a breakout session of a child sexual abuse survivor. I can't call her a victim because she has transcended all of those bad memories. She said she had struggled for many years and finally she came to a place of enlightenment.

She said that someone told her to think of all experiences, good or bad, from a different perspective. So now when things get bad, she thinks of this scenario. First she imagines spirits dancing around in a spirit world, being carefree and just enjoying each other. Then she sees The Great Spirit strive in the mist. He says: "I need" and before he can say another word, all the little spirits volunteer.

He laughs and says, "No, now let me tell you what I need." After that the spirits listen intently. He continues: "I need someone to go to this family. They have forgotten and I need someone to remind them." He says: "You will have interesting experiences but two things will never change: (1) I will never leave you; and (2) when it is all over, you can always come home." Then He asked again: "Now who is willing to go?" And again, every hand in the spirit world goes up. Why, because they all know this to be true.

Somehow, once we get here on Earth, we are separated from the truth or else we don't recognize it anymore.

Another memory is when I was seven or eight months old. I had on a white T-shirt and a white cloth diaper. I was standing on my father's lap. He was holding my two arms/hands up and I was trying to walk. We were sitting on the side of the bed. It seemed to be in the evening, so I can surmise that we were getting ready for bed. My mother was sitting next to him, leaning on him. This memory is very "all of us were laughing." It is a very happy memory.

I couldn't tell if it was morning, noon or night. Most of this memory has faded over the years. But what I felt has not faded. I felt loved, protected and I especially remember my father's voice. He was encouraging me to walk. I knew that he had my hands and that he would hold me up. I wasn't scare or anything. My mother was encouraging me also, but I definitely remember the tone of my father's voice. He had a deep voice, very manly.

Over the years I would come to associate this voice with terror, then sadness, then pain, and finally grief.

My next memory was when I was two years and seven months old. My sister had just been born. My sister was a few weeks old in this memory.

My mother was carrying my sister and my aunt, my mother's older sister, was holding my hand and walking me to a train. My aunt lifted me onto the train and then she lifted me onto a seat. My mother sat down next to me holding my new baby sister. She was all wrapped up.

Now I know I was in Birmingham, Alabama, where my mother went to give birth to my sister and me. She left our father up North and she went to her sister's house to have her babies. Both of our birth certificates verify that. This was a time where I felt secure and well adjusted.

My sister, who was borne right after me was the last one of the siblings to be born there. The other six siblings were born in the northern city where we lived. Over the next few years, six others would be added. But even though there were more mouths to feed, sometimes two separate siblings were added in the same year, one in January and one in December. Our accommodations did not "grow" with our family. We lived in very tight quarters for a very long time.

Yes, obviously I am from a very large family. I am the eldest of eight children by my mom and dad. Both had children before they came together, so I have older siblings who I know very well and love very much. Some of the older siblings I didn't meet until my teenage years. But we still maintain a strong friendship and bond today.

I believe this is probably from my father's influence. My father had a saying about "half" sisters and brothers. He would say what is a half-sister of brother? He would ask if they were half a person? We would say no, because we knew them to be whole people. Then he would say: "They may have a different mother or a different father, but they are still your brothers and sisters." And that's how we were raised.

And speaking about my dad, he was a complicated man, and from that we had a complicated relationship. He was the product of being born and raised in the deep, segregated South, on a sharecropper's plantation with lynching, beatings, Jim Crow, and unmitigated fear. So when he got the chance he left physically, but he could never get past the ghost of his past, which haunted him until the day he died.

And even though he was able to make it North, the scars bled mightily, especially when he drank heavily, which was every weekend. He worked as a common laborer because he had no certifiable skill set. He could barely read and write, but he was mighty strong and powerfully built. Many people would pick a fight with him because he was gruff and tough, but they usually got the short end of the stick. He was known for his legendary strength. One day, folks said he lifted the front end of an old car by himself.

I have never known my father to use his strength to hurt anyone. But that strength caused many people to want to hurt him. Most times on weekends, when his buddies got sauced, they would try to "take him."

In those days, just like now, you needed to have something that made you different, that made you unique. Or you would be born, live and die as a farm hand, on a sharecropper's land with no chance of escape.

He told us very little about his life, but this is what I know for sure. His mother was only fourteen years old when she had him. He was his mother's only child with the man we called Grandpa. Grandpa worked his entire life for the railroad, forty-two years. He was not literate but he was thrifty. Over the years, he accumulated a small fortune in real estate. He only had one daughter with his wife and Grandpa stayed in close contact with her all his life, unlike his relationship with my father. As a result, I only saw Grandpa twice in my life.

I saw Grandpa once when I was traveling with my husband on a road trip to Florida. Suddenly I saw the sign on the expressway with the name of the town where he lived. An inexplicable feeling came over me to see this gentleman, so we just had to delay our plans. We were running late to rendezvous with other couples in Florida and we still had a couple of hundred miles to go—but I didn't care. I was almost in tears for the longing I had to see my paternal grandfather. It was unexplainable. I didn't have an address or anything. I just knew I needed to stop and see him.

Finally, my husband pulled off the highway onto a dusty road. Then he looked at me and said: "What next?" I got the brilliant idea to go to the City Hall. Most of those little towns had a city hall where everybody knew everybody. This town was no different. I mounted the stairs and went to the clerk's desk. A Caucasian deputy asked me if he could help me? I told him I was looking for my grandfather and I told him who my grandfather was. He told me where my grandfather was probably hanging out, with the older gentlemen of his age. I told the deputy I had never been there before and he gave me explicit directions on how to find Grandpa. And find him I did!

He was at the funeral home, sitting outside, shooting the breeze with his cronies. He was very glad to see my husband and me. He said he knew about me and the other siblings and was surely glad he got to lay eyes on one of us before he died. So I tried to bring him up to date about me and my sisters and brothers. He knew my older siblings very well because they had grown up thirty miles down the road in another town, the town my father was born in, Millbrook, Alabama.

After a brief visit, we left him with a promise that we would visit again. And I kept that promise. Almost ten years later, I went to a family reunion on my father's side. It probably took me this long to return because my father never returned.

My father was born after slavery but during the midst of Jim Crow. His life was hard—and I do mean hard. He picked cotton, chopped wood, cleared fields, etc., all day long, all week long, with no end in sight.

This was during the WWII era. Many of his male cousins escaped through the Draft, or joined the Army before they were drafted. This just didn't sit right with my father. On the one hand, his family would get an allotment from the Army, which would come in handy to make ends meet. On the other hand, he rationalized that he might get killed, and he figured he would stay right where he was and take his chances with lynch mobs rather than die on some foreign soil. So he waited until he received his draft letter. Rumor said he began to eat soap so he would fail the physical. And guess what? He failed the physical. He never saw a day of in the Armed Services.

I have been to the "family home" on many occasions. But I didn't get to the South until I was a grown woman. My parents made a hard choice in leaving segregation, looking for a better life in the North. All I can surmise is that it was a tremendous struggle to just stay alive, just subsist in that environment.

Unfortunately, I don't know much more of my paternal grandmother. She came to town a couple of times and stayed with us for a few short days. But her visit made an indelible mark on my life because of the relationship between her and my dad, her son.

It seems he didn't know his mother was coming to town on one of those occasions. But it just so happened that the day she arrived, my father was arrested for disorderly conduct while drinking and taken to our county jail. When we got the call, my mother had to ask a neighbor for bail money. My father knew she didn't have any money, but yet he called begging for her to please, *please* come and get him.

My mother asked an elderly, fatherly gentlemen whom we knew very well and he gave her the money. He was raising his grandson and he lived in the tenement building right next door. He reminded me a lot of my father—big and commanding. I once saw him stomp a rat to death in the yard between our buildings. It was a big, black "river rat" as we called them. They were everywhere and as tenants our biggest worry. We neighborhood children were outside playing because our tenements were just too unbearably hot to be in. It was the heat of summer, but it was pretty late at night. Normally that is the time when the rats come out of hiding, foraging for food. This rat was just unlucky that night. After this gentleman killed him, he held him up by his tail. He was at least twelve inches long, body alone!

After my mother received the money, she walked the five city blocks to the jailhouse and secured my father's release. He would not be released immediately but had to be "processed out," and that would take a while. So my mother walked back home in the pitch black, by herself, to await his return. She was not allowed to see him, so he had no way of knowing his mother was in town.

Soon thereafter, my father walked in. He was quite angry and upset. I don't know exactly if he was one or if he was both. I do know he started fussing and cussing at my mother as soon as he put the key in the door. He stormed through our house, throwing things and calling my mother every vile, despicable name he could think of. And just think, she had just bailed him out of jail.

My grandmother took all she could take. Then she emerged from the bedroom. In those days, we only had three rooms—a kitchen, which had a fold-out, roll-away cot in it; a living room that had a couple of let-out couches; and a bedroom, which had one full-sized bed. Eight people stayed in these rooms each and every day, two adults and six children—and now my grandmother.

As soon as my father saw his mother, he began to apologize profusely. She looked at him with pity in her eyes and she called him by his name. She admonished him with one sentence. She said: "I didn't raise you like this." Then she asked him:

"What happened to you?" She said, "Your wife came and got you out, and this is how you treat her?" She told him to think of his little children, who by then were all awake, scared and looking at this exchange between mother and son. Our father, who was normally in charge, was cowering in the face of his mother.

He was the eldest of seven children and was raised by his grandmother. She was one-hundred percent Indian. One day, she walked off the reservation, onto the plantation, and married his grandfather, a black slave. My father called her "Ma." Because he and his fourteen-year-old mother was raised in the same house with his grandmother until his mother married. His biological father never married his mother, and he had a sister on his father's side who he kept in touch with all of his life. I wouldn't understand a lot of this until I was grown, had extensive conversations with my aunts, and had children and grandchildren of my own. A lot of this oral history did not come from my father's lips, but rather from my paternal aunts, because my father couldn't speak through the pain. I would later come to realize that my own choices and marital circumstances would mirror my father's pain.

I knew my father's life was hard. But I had no idea how hard until he got word that his mother had died. Since he was the eldest, everyone came to our house to wait for my father. When he got off of work, he returned home just like he usually did when it was not the weekend. He knew something was wrong when he saw the house full. Then my mother told him the sad news.

I had never seen my father cry anytime in my life, but I witnessed this scene of sorrow that I would replay many times in my life. My hero, my father, was a broken man over the death of his mother. I head him say through his river of free falling tears: "Now I have no one." I didn't understand what he meant then. Now I know grief can be such a crushing blow, that you are left reeling, wondering how you can even continue to breathe?

My father had not been back home in forty years. That night, I found out why. He had left in the middle of the night for fear of lynching. A prosperous Caucasian family owned the only grocery store in town. The owner's son had insisted that my grandmother had not paid for something in his store. My grandmother was telling him that yes, she had paid for it and this exchange went on for while—and it was becoming heated.

Presently, my father came down the street. He saw his mother in the store and she was very agitated and distraught. He asked them both what the problem was. First the owner told my father that my grandmother owed a debt that had not been settled yet. Then my grandmother told my father that yes, she had paid that specific debt on this specific date with these specific funds, for this specific amount. At that moment it is said that my father jumped the counter, grabbed the owner's son and told him, "Now you listen here. If she said she paid that debt, then #%$+&^&*#*& she paid the debt, so leave her alone!"

That night the local establishment came to supposedly have a talk with my father. They were going to teach that "nigger" who was in charge and put him in his place once and for all. I understand it was a lynch mob and they came to grandmother's house.

Lucky for my father, he was already gone. When you live in a place, you know the rhyme and rhythm of that place. You know its ebbs and flows. You know what is acceptable behavior and what will not be tolerated. My father's behavior could not be tolerated or the entire town might rise up. So they came to nip it in the bud so to speak.

My father left with all the money he could get his hands on. It wasn't much, just the change everyone had in his or her pockets. He had said his goodbyes and he had promised to keep in touch. About the time the mob showed up, all tears had been dried and my grandmother looked them in their eyes and said: "He's not here and I don't know where he is." Thank God they took her at her word after they had searched the house and the surrounding area. But they left an admonition: "If he should show up, tell him we are looking for him and we will find him." Everyone in this town knew his life was in danger, he most of all.

So he hopped a train going north. And when he could get off, he tried to buy a train ticket to some friends way up North, but he didn't have enough money. So he bought one right across the Mason Dixon Line. Now in some places, this is considered the Ohio River. That is not the true Mason Dixon Line, but for him it would suffice. He was able to find a job doing hard manual labor right away. Because he was strong and in excellent shape, he was able to survive many hardships, including having his heart broken by having to leave his family.

Now, he had to make a decision if he was going to return for his mother's funeral. In the South, memories are long and patience is short. He wanted to return for his mother's funeral, but he didn't want to be put in jail or worst, lynched. So his initial reaction was to say he wasn't going back. The next day some of his cousins stopped over to tell us the offending family had said it was all right for him to return. They would not prosecute him or accost him in any way. But he didn't trust them. He knew them too well.

I could say that he never went back, but he did go back for his father's funeral. A remarkable thing happened leading to his death and afterward. I have finally put it all in perspective. My grandfather had called us about a year before he died. He told my father he was going to leave him a considerable amount of land. My father stated emphatically that he didn't want it. We found out later that it was left to his children instead. Walmart came along years later and wanted to buy the property. Each of his children had to sign off on it. We were tricked into signing it by his half-sister and our older sister.

They told us it was for an old man who had nothing. Surely we signed not knowing we signed away our heir property. But that just goes to show you how much my father disliked the South and the terrible memories that haunted him.

Suffice it to say, he was my first "love." As I grew older, I began to know there were different types of love for different people. I was always trying to get his attention. But with so many mouths to feed and no guaranteed way to feed them, his life was hard and so was ours.

I had a skewed vision of my father, that he could move mountains; but my mother knew the truth of his flailing dysfunction.

He had immature coping skills and he never had a good role model. They tell us, he came to live with his mother and stepfather when he was a teenager. His stepfather beat his mother. One day, he intervened and for this heroic act, he was cast out of the home house, left to fend for himself. So he became a survivor, by any means necessary.

When I remember him, I remember a voice that was deep and rumbling. He was a big, powerful, loud and boisterous man. He would fill up any room he walked into.
He would come into the house, in the middle of the night from a night of drinking and carousing, and he would wake us up cussing and fussing. On the one hand, we were glad our daddy was home, but one the other hand, whenever he was there, he was fussing and cussing.

He has not once ever told us he loved us, or he was proud of us, or anything complimentary. In fact, he would give us all nicknames based on some physical flaw or personality characteristic. And he would use those hurtful names in "mixed" company. His theory was to embarrass us to make us tough because he believed you had to be tough to survive in this world.

As I got older, I once asked him why he cursed so much and why didn't he ever go to church with us? I really don't remember what his answer was. But later, I heard that he was a deacon at his home church down South. He told us that his mother cursed every third word that came out of her mouth and so did his stepfather. And guess what, his brother and sister also do the same thing. He also told us that each and every weekend his parents would throw a party at their house when he was growing up there. That is where he learned to drink, cuss and play cards.

It is funny because now we realize that even though the entire lot of them swore like sailors, they definitely loved us and we loved them.

I was grown when I got this revelation. I remember once when I was a teenager and going through a particularly difficult phase, I told my mother that I feared our daddy didn't love us. She tried to assuage my fears, but how I felt was based on his words and actions. Finally, in the heat of the moment, when I was again a rebellious teenager, I told him I knew he didn't love me. I can't even remember how or if he answered me. But I do know now that yes, he did love us; yes, he was proud of us; and yes, he came to my rescue many times and in many ways over the course of his lifetime.

Now I know you are probably wondering about my mother. She was there through it all. If his and mine was a complicated relationship, there must not be a word in our language to describe their relationship. No, she could not protect herself from his abuses, so you know she couldn't protect us.

We asked her why she stayed and put up with his abuses. She told us that she didn't have an identifiable skill set and she had nowhere to go. My mother was the youngest of four children, who was also raised by her grandmother. She was a God-fearing, Christian woman who demanded respect from everyone but her husband. Her husband left her every October and lived with a woman during the winter and early spring, and every time he came back home to her, she let him back into the house.

My grandmother was considered a "loose woman," and although she had four children, she didn't have time to raise them. She left them with her elderly mother, our God-fearing great grandmother.

This is what my mother saw, heard and learned. She never was empowered. She had no good role model. Her mother was always "in the streets" and her grandmother was always talking down about men. Look at this dichotomy. So she had varying opinions about adult relationships. As I look back now, I shake my head at some of the advice she gave us about men, growing up, etc. And here is why my mother never felt empowered.

THE TALE OF TWO SISTERS

What if the worst thing that could every happen to you, happened to you? Who would you turn to? Who could help you? This is what happened to my mother and her older sister. Both were brutally raped. I am not sure if the third sister was raped also. This was something that should never happen to anyone, and it happened to two sisters in the same family and at different times.

The older sister, my aunt, lost her ability to have children and almost lost her life. She was brutally raped when she was following her aunt to the mailbox. On the sharecroppers' plantation, where they lived, you had to walk up to the paved road to retrieve your mail. It was not delivered to your shack. It still is not delivered to your address. You still have to walk up to the post office to retrieve it. Between the shacks and the post office was a large field of high grass. My aunt told me she was taken by a boy of age sixteen, and she was just nine years old.

When he turned her loose, she stumbled home. Her mother saw her and told her to go to bed, and then the bleeding would stop. But it didn't. Her father came in and heard what happened. When he saw his oldest daughter, lying in a pool of blood, he picked her up and carried her to their old wagon. (This wagon was pulled by a stubborn mule, which would eventually kill my grandfather by stomping him in his chest.) And he took her to the only doctor in town who would treat black people back then.

My grandfather was industrious, and he made moonshine back up in the woods back then. He was known for having the best moonshine in those parts. So he had money to pay for the treatment of his daughter. After the doctor did his examination and patched her up as best he could, he told my grandfather two things: (1) that she would live and (2) that she would never be able to bear children; and he was right on both accounts.

Word got around about what happened. In small towns it is hard to keep anything a secret. Nothing was ever done to that young man.

My mother also knew her attacker and to this day she has never forgiven him. She has a very tangible reminder of the horrific abuse she suffered—a son, my eldest brother. It has affected my brother in profound ways also. He knows his father's name and about 15 years ago, he found out he was living in the same city with us. My mother never speaks his name. But my brother asked my aunt and myself to contact this man because my brother wanted to finally meet his biological father.

That gentleman's response to our query was a resounding NO! My mother and brother don't have much of a relationship. Every time she looks at him, she sees and feels the old hurt and misery resurface. In fact we knew nothing about him until he showed up at our house when he was a young man. My older brother was raised in a Southern state by my mother's sister his aunt. His existence was miserable. My aunt was a single parent trying to raise two children of her own. My mother eventually had another child, a daughter whom my aunt also was given to raise.

And to add insult to injury, our older brother was rejected by his biological father. He is rather bitter, quick tempered and quite judgmental. He wears a chip on his shoulder. It's like he won't let anyone get to really know him for fear of being hurt. He has some serious abandonment issues. Just as soon as he got old enough, he grabbed his sister and they fled up North. He sent his sister to college while he worked several jobs. His father passed away in a domicile for veterans without once laying eyes on the son he had fathered through a brutal rape.

My uncle (their brother) had some extra money when he came home from the Army. The first thing he did was buy my mother a ticket to visit her sister in the North. That visit became a lifelong stay. She never went back South to live, but she did go back to visit every ten to fifteen years.

How do you show love to people who have never been loved? How can you expect love from someone who doesn't know how to love? I know my mother doesn't truly love herself, so she was incapable of loving us. She never learned how to love herself unconditionally like God loved us. To this day, she still harbors secrets and has never, ever forgiven my daddy, who has been dead now for over twenty years. She really doesn't realize that she had the power to change her situation all along. She was the enabler and she still is. She doesn't know how to set boundaries and she says she is too old now to learn.

God doesn't call the equipped, He equips the called!

I am convinced that when we are babes in knowledge, He changes our circumstances. And when we become mature in knowledge, He changes us.

If God takes you to the top of the mountain and tells you to jump, one of two things is going to happen. Either He will be there to catch you or He will teach you to fly. It has been the journey of learning how to fly that has been the greatest joy of my life. Even though it has been painful, the journey has been worth it.

Lessons learned from The Love Movement of My Life:

1. Love doesn't always look like what we think it should look like.
2. We can't let mainstream media dictate what love is or what love isn't.
3. God is love and He loves all of us.
4. To be moved by love, you must be able to communicate in love.
5. The power of forgiveness

CHAPTER 2

The Power of Twelve

When Jesus was twelve years old, he went with his parents and other members of his community, on a journey to Jerusalem for the Passover. They did this every year. But this year signaled a change for Jesus.

After the Passover celebration, all started out walking back to their homes, which was customary. After walking for three days, his parents noticed that he was not with the crowd heading back home. They immediately became alarmed and turned around, heading back to Jerusalem to find their son.

After searching for him frantically, they found him in the temple, talking with the elders. The elders were amazed at his knowledge and his interpretation of the Old Testament scriptures. His parents scolded him, telling him that they had been very worried about him once they discovered that he was not with them.

His response was: "Didn't you know that I would be in My Father's House?" "Didn't you know I had plans the world knew nothing about?" "I am about My Father's business." He was the tender age of twelve.

The question becomes, were the Sanhedrin Council and elders in the temple teaching him or was he teaching them?

Twelve years old is a year of transition. In the Jewish tradition they do a bar mitzvah (as the twelve year old turns thirteen) and in African tradition, they do a manhood ceremony. The Bible says: "When I was a child, I thought like a child and spoke as a child. But when I became an adult, I put away childish things." (Paraphrased)

My twelfth year was a transitional year for me also. I was in the sixth grade and we were studying Egypt. I believe that was a year of profound learning. I also believed the Egyptian culture/civilization is remarkable in so many ways. Their contributions still exist today and are a testament to its impact on this Earth.

Once, while I was in the sixth grade, when studying the Pyramids and the Sphinx, I said to no one in particular that I wanted to visit this land. I still remember the riddle of the "Sphinx" and the Oedipus complex. I hid that desire in my heart for a while but then forgot about them. However, I believe that God never forgot. It would be thirty-six years later when I stepped off a barge onto the shore in Cairo, Egypt. I had just floated down the Nile River. All I can say is God never forgot my dream. I grew up and forgot about my dream. Life happened, but God is faithful.

While touring the Pyramids, our tour guide asked if anyone knew the riddle of the Sphinx and I said I did. So he asked me to tell the rest of the group and I did. I didn't stumble. I was not afraid. I didn't hesitate. I rose to the occasion.

And in case you are wondering what the riddle is, it goes like this: "What walks on four legs in the morning, two legs at noon and three legs in the evening." The answer is a human— during the three stages of life: infancy, adulthood and old age.

Some other things happened to me that was very significant. The Sunday, before my twelfth birthday, I "joined" our church. After Sunday School on that particular Sunday, we moved to the main sanctuary. I stood in front of the entire church and confessed my hope in Christ. I was eleven years old. The very next Saturday, I turned twelve years old. The day after my twelfth birthday was Easter Sunday. It came early that year. The next Sunday was first Sunday and that was the Sunday I had my baptism. I was submerged in our baptism pool. Then we took Communion. My mother was crying. My sisters and brothers wondered what the big deal was. I was happy.

Later on that year our school did the opera, *Amahl and The Night Visitors*. We did this opera every year and it was a big deal. Those who were chosen for the speaking parts were excused from class and got to go to rehearsal in the main auditorium. There were songs to be learned and costumes to be made. Also, around this same time, for the very first time, our community radio station invited us to do the opera on the radio. Our school needed someone to narrate the entire program and the rest of the school would sing the songs. Guess whom they selected to be the narrator? That's right, yours truly.

Some of the teachers coached me day and night. They really invested themselves into getting me ready for that special day. Because of their time and attention, the program went off without a hitch. My performance was lauded as memorable, which was unusual for a twelve-year-old child. I was not afraid. I didn't hesitate. I rose to the occasion.

The lesson I learned is: Past associations and relationships will prepare you for future developments. Your associations will prepare you for your destiny. God will give you "uncommon" knowledge of "uncommon" things in "uncommon" time for an "uncommon" destiny.

Another lesson I learned is: Your gifts will develop at an early age if given the right environment. I was nurtured, encouraged and supported. God will place the right people in your life. Sometimes God will place teachers, leaders and guides in your life, but He will call you personally.

The incident at the Pyramids was a setup for a big step up! God showed me my future before my beginnings. Rough starts produce roots. Strong roots produce good fruit.

CHAPTER 3

Life Happens

I have had many "firsts" in my life, but one first really stands out for me. During my sophomore year, a program which was funded by the government at the national level and was called "Upward Bound." Its aim was to take students who might have had some college potential and motivate, support and guide them into college. It encompassed sophomore, junior and senior years.

I was just like any other teenager, excited about my first paying job, at age sixteen. In my sophomore year, I had secured a coveted position for summer, seasonal employment with the United State Postal Service. I would be working forty hours per week and would be compensated at the rate of sixty dollars per week for twelve weeks. In those days, that was a lot of money for a teenager working a summer job. And I knew just want I would do with that money. Some would go to help out with my family. Some would go to buy myself much needed school clothes and school supplies. And some portion I would save.

I was always pretty active in our community and always went to our community center. I would always avail myself of the opportunity to read a book or newspaper at the center. One day, when I was there, I was introduced to a college professor from our local university. She was starting a new program in our city called Upward Bound.

She explained the premise of the program to me. After we discussed all the nuances of this program, she asked me a *big* question. She asked if I wanted to be a part of this program. She said that we would get a stipend every month, plus we would live on the college campus for six weeks during the summer. She said we would get help with homework during the week. But the best thing she said was we would get to travel to other colleges inside and outside the state. This is similar to the college tours they have now. A guarantee that I would be accepted into our college after graduation seemed like a consolation prize behind travel.

She told me if I were accepted into the program, I would be the first of sixty students that would be enrolling that inaugural year. She said she would have to contact my school, community partners and she would need permission from my parents. And that is when the proverbial shoe dropped.

My parents were happy for me to have summer employment. They were also glad that I would be able to buy my own supplies. That would be one less mouth to feed and one less child to clothe. So how did I break the news to them?

I distinctly remember, when I told my mom that I wanted to go to Upward Bound that summer and not to work at the Post Office, she was very supportive. My father, on the other hand, pitched a hissy fit. He said I needed to go to work because I needed the money.

Guess which one I did that summer? I became the first Upward Bound student in our hometown. About ten years ago, I was honored as being the first student enrolled in our city's Upward Bound program. And to this day, the director of the program—yes the one who I met that day—still maintains a close friendship with me. I was at her 90th birthday party along with others with whom she still keeps in touch.

Remember I told you earlier that my family lived in very close, cramped quarters? Well, my senior year of high school, I decided to leave my parents house and strike out on my own. It was a difficult year for me. I had to couch surf. I had to find and keep a job with no skill set. I had to stay in school if I ever wanted to graduate. And I had to navigate all the things that normal teenagers navigate.

I got through one of the most tumultuous years of my life. I graduated on time but didn't have enough money to buy my class ring or go to the prom. Besides, no one asked me. No, I was not very popular. But I did learn how to wait tables and earn tips. I also learned how to depend on me and me alone.

I made a friend in high school who would walk with me during the next forty-five years. She was the wind beneath my wings. She was my cheering section, always abounding in love. She played clarinet and was in the marching band. We both tried out for choir but I made it and she didn't. Then I tried out for our special ensemble and I made that also. I had sung a solo in church when I was twelve. That was the extent of my singing career.

My friend studied shorthand, where I loved science. She could cook while I loved to sew. You see, we were opposites but we complemented each other.

Love called her home a couple of years ago, but I still keep in touch with her mother, her father and her children. I get invited to all the family functions.

I guess I earned this privilege in more ways than one. In my first year of Upward Bound, I became friends with several people who lived in my neighborhood who were also in Upward Bound that year. That very next school year, I told my friend about a gentleman in our program. As life would have it, my friend joined Upward Bound that same year. I introduced these two and the rest, as they say, is history. They met, fell in love, got married and had several children.

My own life was not so predictable. I did go to college right after high school, but I flunked out after two semesters. I became depressed because of life circumstances. I would find myself lying in bed all morning, all noon and night. I skipped classes and generally hung out in my room.

Inevitably, this same lady who was the director of Upward Bound came to my dorm room, packed up my belongings and brought me back to my parent's house. What a humiliating experience that was. But

I stayed there for about a year. After that, I felt that same old restlessness inside of me telling me: It is time to go. And go I went. I found a menial government job with good benefits and I stayed on this job for the next five years.

I also met my first husband on this job. We were part of a "pilot program." This institution hired about twenty young people, myself included, taught us a skill and gave us an opportunity to prove ourselves. This set the stage for my future.

A nurse from the Air Force taught us. She made health care exciting.

I had worked as a candy striper at our Veterans hospital for about a month when I was fifteen years old. I remember the sights, sounds, smells, but it didn't turn me off. I was young and looking for something glamorous to do with my life and that definitely was not glamorous. I had sewn all of my clothes in my senior year. I figured I could be a fashion designer. But I really only considered that career choice for a nanosecond.

My first husband and I kind of backed into each other. We started hanging out. Then we got into a routine. Since we both were from church-going families, we figured we better get married or burn in hell.

We didn't understand what marriage entailed. Again, neither one of us had good role models. We didn't know anyone who had a successful, long-term marriage. In those days, they didn't require marriage counseling at my home church. So we chose a ring, chose a date and had a big church wedding. Besides, everyone around us was getting married including my BFF No. 1.

At this company, I met another woman who would become my BFF number 2. We are still best friends today. She was my maid of honor at my wedding. Before my husband and I got married, he quit this job to pursue another career goal. As I was planning my wedding, I finished an associate degree at our area junior college. After I got married, I quit that position to try to find something in my field. We bought our first house and I also got pregnant right away.

The pregnancy was uneventful. My husband painted the nursery blue. In those days, we didn't have sonograms to know the sex of the baby before they were born. But somehow we just knew it would be a boy.

We always said my Mother missed her calling. She had the uncanny ability to look at each one of us, early in our pregnancy, and be able to tell you the sex of the baby. Right now she is batting a thousand! We figured she gets what she wants. It doesn't matter what you want (or you better want what she wants because she always gets what she wants.)

I was due on December 10th. I figured by Christmas, I could go to church. Wrong. I figured I could wear something I already had in my closet. Wrong again. By Christmas,

I still hadn't delivered. So my obstetrician told me to come into the office the day after Christmas, which I did. After examining me, he told me that the baby would come when it was suppose to and not to worry or try to rush it. He was concerned that since this was my first pregnancy, one of us might have miscalculated.

I was one miserable soul. I tried everything anyone told me to get the baby to come. I tried mall walking, eating hot sauce with everything, even taking hot baths, but to no avail. Finally, I sent my husband to the drug store for some over the counter medicine. I got in labor that day. I waited to call my ob-gyn and just as I thought, he didn't believe me. Instead of telling me to go to the hospital, he told me to come to the office so he could examine me himself.

Upon examination, he immediately picked up the phone and called the hospital for a direct admit. Then things began to happen very fast. I had taken Lamaze classes with my BFF, so I immediately called her.

She arrived in short order and me, her and my husband began the arduous task of bringing forth this life.

Finally after what seemed like hours of pushing, I was wheeled into the delivery room. But wait a minute. Something was happening or something was not happening. After a while, I was taken back to the labor room and hooked to an IV, a Pitocin drip. This is one of the most dreaded and feared medications for women who are getting ready to deliver. It pushes you into full-fledged labor. I was also put on oxygen to help the baby breathe.

The baby was getting into some distress. Thirty more minutes of hurting, pushing, feeling pain like you have never felt before, and still nothing. This is truly where the doctor's skill comes into play. He made the painful decision to give me a C-section. My mother and my husband's mother were called. I was given a spinal block. I heard everyone talking, but I was having a private conversation with my God.

I was asking God to please let me die, right then and right there. I knew my baby would be loved and well taken care of. I didn't believe a human being could stand that sort of pain and continue to live. I had hit my breaking point and it would be almost twenty years before I would begin to feel normal again.

Suffice it to say, I started with postpartum blues later during that hospital stay. I hit postpartum depression and before it was all over, I would have full-blown psychosis. We know a lot more about what happens to a woman's body during childbirth now, but in those days, nobody suspected the chaos my mind and body was in.

I stayed in the hospital for eight days. They didn't let me hold the baby unless someone was in the room with me. I didn't comb my hair, didn't brush my teeth. I just didn't want to live. But God looked past my faults and He saw my needs. He was the only one who saw my needs. My own husband said:

"Nobody had a baby and lost their mind." Oh, but I did.

Within two years, I was admitted to the psychiatric ward for a nervous breakdown. I also joined the ranks of the newly divorced. But by that time, I had a decent job with a Fortune 500 company, with good benefits. I was still connected to my home church, still connected to my family and friends. Even though I was struggling, I can look back and see how Love found a way when all hope was lost.

CHAPTER 4

Descent into Chaos

Most people cannot point to a single moment in time when they cross the point of no return. You could say it was the traumatic birth of my first child. But I would say that you were probably wrong.

I believe I was born depressed. I have suffered from some degree of depression most of my life. I was not aware of it until I graduated from high school. Maybe up until that time, I led a sheltered life and didn't really have to deal with the realities. But after high school and that half-year of college at our major university, life got very real.

I was always just a mediocre student. I didn't push myself very hard. I always felt like I had nothing to prove to anyone. I was a whiz at English and a complete failure at math, but I loved science. I also was pretty creative. Plus I could sing, or so I thought. I figured these qualities would get me through whatever I would face in life.

I have never felt the need to belong to anything. When everyone else was rushing for a sorority, I was reading a book. This habit of always having a book handy would serve me well my entire life. I am still an avid reader. I will read anything and everything. I will devour everything I can put my hands on. Reading is therapeutic for me. It is the greatest opiate I know.

I moved out of my parents' home into one room across town. Then I heard that my high school had become a junior college and I could go there for a much more reduced rate than our main university. I investigated their offerings. In hindsight, I wanted to say that I should have studied something else other than Medical Assisting. But what made that program unique was upon graduation, you would receive an Associate Degree.

Wow, that would be something, an Associate Degree. That sounded wonderful. I would be the first one in my family to finish college with a degree, even if it was an associate's. So along with my full-time employment, I started a full-time program at our junior college.

I won't tell you it was easy. But I will tell you that it was worth it in the long run. I did graduate with an Associate Degree in Medical Assisting. I quit my government employment and went job hunting. By this time I had gotten married, so I didn't have to worry so much about money. And within one year of marriage, we bought a house and had a beautiful baby boy.

By this time, my husband was an over-the-road truck driver. I remember coming home to tell him he had full-time responsibility for our child because I was checking myself into a private mental hospital. I felt that I just couldn't go on. I had to have some help or I would kill myself.

He had to take vacation for the week I was away. He never came to visit.

I had group therapy, one-on-one therapy, milieu therapy with medication therapy. I began to feel better, but I was on a psychiatric drug that made me sleepy and made me gain a lot of weight. But I wasn't worried about the weight. I was worried about me.

My best friends didn't want to talk about my recent hospitalization. I can only surmise that their way of dealing with my situation was to not discuss it and maybe it would go away. After a while I was able to act normal and I went looking for another position.

I found one at our local Fortune 500 company. It was in part because I had an Associate Degree. By this time, my husband and I were living two very separate lives but living under the same roof. It was no communication unless we said something about our son.

No one can live like that and continue to call it a marriage. Eventually we separated, which led to an amicable divorce. Here I was a young woman with a baby and a house note. This was not the life I had envisioned for myself.

I lived next door to a couple who had several children around my age. Our houses were very close together and they kind of kept a watch over my child and myself. One day, their eldest son came over and told everyone that his wife had just given birth to their second child, a girl. Their first child was a boy.

My heart ached so bad for another child that I ran into the house, stood at the kitchen sink, turned on the water and cried my heart out. I didn't want anyone to know how much I wanted another child. I had to be ridiculous since I was a divorcee with no prospects.

They always say, be careful what you ask for because you just might get it.

My BFF number 2 was out one night shortly after this incident and she met two gentlemen. She has always been more mature than I was. I could always trust her judgment. So when she called and said she had met two men and one would be a good fit for me, I was excited. She suggested that me, her and another girl go out the next weekend, to the same spot and perhaps he would return.

I got my family to babysit, put on my clothes and went out with them. As life is sometimes stranger than fiction, he did walk through the door after we had been there for an hour. But he didn't say one word to me. He spoke to my friend he had met last week and sat down next to the other young lady who was with us. My girlfriend kicked me under the table as a signal I had better do something quick before this situation took an ugly turn. She indicated I had better make some type of move or it would be too late.

I had never been one to think quickly on my feet, but this night was going to be an exception. I totally ignored him and focused all my attention on her. I first asked her if she was getting sleepy since it was getting late and she said no. Next, I asked

her if she had the beginnings of a headache, and she agreed that she did. Then I told her it was pretty late and she probably needed to be heading home since she was driving herself and she lived on the other side of town. She agreed with me and left promptly after that.
They always say hindsight is twenty-twenty. And looking back on this incident, I probably should have been the one to leave and not her. But I didn't.

That gentleman became the father of my two other children and my husband in that order.

This gentleman was very intelligent with a very good job. He was in middle management. These were the very qualities I was looking for in a husband. Plus he had never been married nor did he have any children. Wow, I felt very lucky. I was riding on cloud nine.

At first our courtship consisted of expensive dinners, concerts, talking late on the phone and gifts. This was the usual stuff relationships are made of. I took him to meet my family and friends. He was such a catch. I probably didn't pay a lot of attention to the fact that he seemed to be uncomfortable around my little son. I probably should have paid attention that he lived a very lavished lifestyle with no savings account. I probably should have paid attention that he had never had a female girlfriend. Is that what he said or was it what I heard? And I should have really paid attention when his mother, aunt, two uncles and a great aunt presumably came to see his children, but really they came to make sure I was a real woman.

The signs were there that this was a troubled young man, but my heart overruled my head. I told my aunt candidly about this gentleman right after my second child, a daughter, was born. She told me to take my babies and get as far away from this man as possible.

My mother on the other hand thought he was Jesus descended from Heaven. This man could do no wrong. We did live a middle class lifestyle. Every Sunday we went to my home church, then out to eat. Next week we would go shopping for extras. We both had nice cars and I could make my house note. He always paid for his two children without questions.

Something in the back of my mind told me I needed to do something with my life. I had always loved health care. But when I worked for this Fortune 500 company, I didn't do anything in health care. But in the back of my mind, I knew I wanted to return. I just didn't know how.

It was frowned upon to be an unwed mother at this company and that is what I became with my second child. I was ridiculed, maligned and finally my boss took me into his office and made me a deal I could not refuse. I ended up leaving the company along with my immediate supervisor who gave me some excellent advice. He said: "This train is so big, you can't rattle the tracks, much less stop the train. The best you can do is get off."

I decided to take his advice.

I went to our "break room" and I started to write a five-page scathing letter of every little hurt that had ever happened to me at that company—and there were lots of them. A colleague came along and asked me what was I doing. I told him I was writing a resignation letter. He stood over my shoulder reading my resignation.

When he had read enough, he snatched the letter from me and crumpled it up and threw it in the trash. He admonished me about my callousness. He told me to rewrite the letter in the standard format. He told me to thank the company for the opportunity to work there and to thank them for the valuable knowledge I had gained. He told me to ask them to wish me well in all future endeavors as I would them.

I did just what he told me to do. It came to one paragraph, not even a half page. But I am here to tell you I got more "mileage" out of that letter than I ever would have gotten from my first letter. I have run into my former managers over the years and we have been very cordial to each other. One year, I was in a position to make a phone call to someone in upper management to help out someone struggling to secure a certain position. This gentleman in upper management had since left the company himself and was heading a very ambitious project which became world famous. I am happy to say the person got the job. I like to think maybe I had just a little bit to do with that.

Since then I have been very cognizant of how "I close a door behind me." I never "bang" it. I close it gently. You never know when you may have to come through that door again. Or another way of saying it is: "Don't burn a bridge that brought you across. You may need it to cross again." That has served me well.

I left that company pregnant with my last child, but I didn't know it. I left on a Friday and started working on finishing my Bachelor's on a

Monday. I took a work-study job to make ends meet. Here I was, working and going to school with two children and one on the way—and still unmarried.

This gentleman had fallen head over heels in love with his first child, a daughter who was born on his thirty-eighth birthday. She adored her father and he adored her. But where did this leave my oldest son by another father? Luckily, he still had a relationship with his father and from time to time, his father would take him to spend the weekend with him. And I tried to spend extra time with him whenever I could.

My mother was the first one to notice that my eldest had a profound sadness about him. She asked if it could be because this gentleman doted on his daughter and ignored my son? I stated emphatically and categorically, "No!" But in the end, she was right.

At age nine months, my daughter was diagnosed with a rare condition. Her small intestine had "telescoped" into her large intestine. Once this diagnosis was confirmed, they scheduled surgery for early the next morning. I called her father from the emergency room and he just told me to keep him informed. It was about three a.m..

She was so exhausted that she was asleep on the bed in our cubicle. We were waiting for the surgeon to arrive. They described the procedure that would involve an incision across her tiny abdomen. By then I had had two C-sections and I knew the inherent risk.

When I looked around, I was all alone with my sick daughter. But the more I thought about it, I didn't want her to have to have surgery. I had to decide what I was going to do about it. So I did the only thing I knew to do. I went to the Great Physician, the One who has never lost a case. He has more healing in the hem of His garment than all the doctors who have ever practiced.

I am glad to say, after that prayer, they wheeled my daughter in for one last X-ray for the surgeon to use in surgery and you know the outcome. The condition had reversed itself and she did not need surgery. They asked me if they could keep her for one more day, just for observation, and I said yes. That was over thirty years ago.

Her father never showed up. But I came and collected my baby the next day, took her home and thanked God for His Grace and His Mercy.

After this, I was on a fast track. I couldn't stay off work or work part time indefinitely, so I gave myself a time frame in which to finish my Bachelor's. Little did I know, I was pregnant with my third child, a boy.

When I was at school or at my work-study job, I knew I was so tired—more tired than was normal—so I made an appointment to see my ob-gyn. Looking back, I wondered why I didn't got to see my primary care specialist.

I told my ob-gyn that I was very tired and that I had been prescribed iron before because of some anemia. He agreed that I was probably just extremely tired since I had a very demanding schedule, two children, school full time, part-time position, etc. But since I was still of childbearing age, he would just do a pregnancy test just to rule it out. When he came back into the room and told me I was pregnant, my first response was visceral. I was livid. I was so angry, I told him that I was not going to let him deliver this baby and stormed out. He just chuckled and told me that was fine but one thing was for sure, I couldn't stay pregnant. Eventually I would have to deliver!

I called the child's father and he was upset also. Things had deteriorated significantly between us. He was no longer speaking to me. He felt like I was trying to trap him. Boy was he ever so wrong! Now I felt like the one who was trapped.

About four months into that pregnancy, my doctors became very alarmed. I had monthly appointments and every time I came in, they would do a test to hear the baby's heartbeat. They were never able to detect one.

Finally the doctor who was going to deliver made the painful decision to terminate the pregnancy. He counseled me and told me sometimes even nature would have an anomaly, something that just didn't go quite right. He said it was probably not a viable fetus and it would never be. It was probably just a mass of tissue.

He told me they were going to bring me into the hospital, admit me and induce labor. Yes, it would be painful but I would be able to have other children. He didn't have to worry about that. That was the last thing on my mind. I had my two children, a boy and a girl, and that was all right with me.

So on the prescribed day, I checked in through the admitting department of the same hospital where I delivered before. Next, I was taken upstairs to labor and delivery. I was given a corner bed so I wouldn't have to hear the other babies crying. How considerate was that?

My doctor came to see me before they started the medicine in an IV drip that would start my labor. After talking with me and making sure I was okay with his decision, he got a funny look on his face. Then he told me that just as a final precaution, he would have the nurse try one more time to find a heartbeat. I lay there thinking thoughts of just how much pain I would have to endure, but in the end it would be worth it and I would most certainly get my tubes tied. I would discuss this with the doctor upon my postpartum visit.

In my reverie, I happened to glance over at the screen and there, just as plain as day, was a genuine, strong, sturdy heartbeat. I didn't know whether to be happy or sad. But I took that as a sign from God that He wanted this child born. I was discharged as soon as the results were communicated to the doctor with a follow-up appointment for the next week.

I finished my class work on a Friday. I took the SAT for grad school on Saturday. I was so big and so miserable that they assigned one proctor for me personally. She had to assist me in going to the restroom and walk with me down the hall. They didn't want anything to happen to me while taking that test.

And I delivered an eight-pound healthy baby boy by C-section that next Wednesday. Again, his father never showed up. He found out that he had a son by calling the patient information line. And when he came to see his son, I hurled a large flowerpot at him. Naturally, this caused a huge commotion. The nurses called my doctor to get an order for restraints and a sedative. My doctor, to his credit, said he wanted to come over and assess me himself first.

He came and I cried a river of tears. I bared my soul to this doctor. He had the best bedside manner or all of the doctors in this practice of seven. He told me he was not going to sedate me nor restrain me, but I couldn't go around hurling flowerpots or I would rip the stitches out from my surgery. I promised to behave myself.

My two other children where staying with my parents. And after the required number of days in the hospital for a healthy mom and babe, we were discharged. I collected my other children and all four of us went home to start a new life.

Part II: Descent into Further Chaos

I made up my mind to raise my three children by myself. I had several friends who were dealing with the same situation. They also had children by men who could not/would not love them because the men themselves had never been loved. They didn't have good role models.

Little did I know, this man's mother was talking with him constantly. She was telling him about right and wrong, about a man's duty to his family. She told him that he couldn't keep having babies without the benefit of marriage. Finally, now I know it was under duress, he asked me to marry him and I said yes. I was ecstatic. My hope and wishes were about to be fulfilled, or so I thought.

We were married in a ceremony in my living room surrounded by close family and our children. We didn't honeymoon. But we made plans to move to a bigger house.

I communicated my happiness to my BFF No. 2—and she warned me. She said I could do better. She told me that he was never going to change.

I told my aunt, my mother's oldest sister, about him. And even though I was "gushing" and skipping over his flaws, she gave me some sage advice. She said: "Honey take your children and get as far away from him as possible. Keep looking forward and leave him behind. He doesn't mean you any good."

Most people who knew us reiterated these same sentiments, all except my mother. By this time, things had deteriorated between us. She thought I was selfish, manipulative and ungrateful. I tried to tell her of the pain this man and situation was causing me. She just couldn't see it. She believed he was the greatest thing since sliced white bread. And she said I was the problem and not him. She would never entertain the fact that he was bisexual. She made me feel that if I could only love him enough, then he wouldn't be attracted to men who dressed and behaved as women.

God kept sending people to me to tell me to just leave. Either I was stubborn, afraid or didn't trust myself or anyone else. It might have been a combination of all of these and other reasons that I didn't name. But I stayed right there and took everything he dished out—the good, the bad and the ugly. Finally God in His Infinite Wisdom spoke to me. I can still hear Him as clearly today as I did when He first said these words to me. They are forever etched in my memory. The words should have changed my life and maybe they did. They certainly set the stage for future decisions that I would make.

God's words to me, which He spoke to my heart that fateful day, were: "This is not who I have for you." And my immediate response was: "But this is who I want." So God said: "OK." Little did I know I had made my bed and now I would have to lie in it.

So as a good little girl who always did what Mommy said do, I buckled down to love him as hard as I could. I would spend days trying to come up with different ways to please him. I cooked his favorite meals, went with him to his favorite clubs, called him during the day and played the good housewife.

And for a time, things would get better, but only to get much worst the very next time we had a disagreement or an argument. I had made up my mind that I was just not going to take any more beatings. I felt like I shouldn't have to. I was his wife and the mother of his children.

He had to attend an "AMEND" program through our local YMCA. This was a program for men who abused women. It was supposed to teach men how to handle their feelings and emotions when they were angry or upset without resorting to violence.

One other thing that probably saved us from any further beatings was I had him removed from our home, through a court order. It was delivered to his job. I didn't want him coming home because he could be very abusive, verbally and physically. I knew if I couldn't protect myself from him, I wouldn't be able to protect my children from him either.

My brother-in-law picked up his clothing and took it to the hotel where he was staying. I didn't know where he was. I just told the children that he was not living with us for a while. Of course my youngest two missed their father.

And after a while, I missed him, too. I had to be mother and father, chauffeur, grass cutter and leaf raker, etc. I had to set out the garbage and do the repairs until the children got older. And I had to work.

Several times he left the house and moved somewhere else, but each time we would reconcile and I would let him back into our home. We never got any counseling, never talked to clergy, etc. We thought we could solve our problems ourselves.

A couple of times, he didn't leave. I left. One time I moved to the YWCA homeless shelter with my three children. We were miserable. We slept in two beds in one room. I had to cook each meal in a common kitchen. We sat around all day except when we talked to the social worker. It was clear to me that this situation wasn't going to work. Besides he had a whole house and we were in a shelter. Something was truly wrong with that picture. I asked the case manager to ask him to leave the house and he agreed. Then we moved back home and the children resumed school. Even though they had been out of school, they quickly made up the time and the assignments.

I had come to depend on him like a wife was supposed to depend on her husband. Even when he was home, he was emotionally detached. And to top this off, he had a very challenging position. His work consumed a lot of time and energy that should have gone to his family.

The school were I had received my Associate Degree had just started a new nursing program. I went and talked with the coordinator and was admitted to the first class. Because I was already working in the field, I would only need to take nursing classes with just a couple of electives to round out my curriculum. Ironically, this program was in my old high school. It had been turned into a junior college. It already had numerous trade and technical programs. This was their newest offering.

This was a dream come true. Every since I had graduated with a Bachelor's and dropped out of grad school after one year toward a Master's, I had been looking for gainful employment. It seemed like every time I applied for a middle management position, they would asked me if I was a nurse and I would have to tell them no. They would tell me that was what they were looking for. So I started the course with the hopes that I would graduate within two years as a registered nurse.

It was a rigorous course of study. I couldn't participate in study groups like some of the younger people in my class. I had to go home and get dinner ready, got to PTA, etc. In my next to last semester, I had a psychology class. It was one of my most challenging classes. I struggled all during that term with grades ranging from D to F. I knew I had to bring my grade point average up to a C or else sit out an entire year and repeat the class.

I was able to do one study group, right before the final exam. We took the final exam at nine a.m. The teacher told us the grades would be available by one p.m. Everyone was invited back at one. I elected to skip going back to class to be humiliated. I just couldn't take receiving my F face to face with all of my classmates knowing my grade. So I called my job as a student nurse and told them I was available for work that afternoon. They were glad to have an extra set of hands and I was glad to get the money.

During my break, I called my teacher to receive my bad news. Again, I found myself making plans as another failure at school. This seemed to be a pattern with me. I wasn't trying to fail on purpose. But try as I might, I just couldn't seemed to graduate.

Instead of the news I expected, I was admonished for not returning with my classmates for the posting of grades and the review. She knew why I didn't return. But she told me I made the highest grade in the class.

She said I set the curve! Wow, I was on cloud nine! That meant that I could return to school next week for the final semester of the program. And I would graduate on time, with my other classmates.

They next quarter was not going to be nearly as hard. We were finished with all the hard courses. That quarter was called "Role Transitions" and getting us ready to take the state board examinations. Besides, I already worked as a student nurse on a cardiac floor. What was any harder than that?

I had applied at that cardiac floor midway through a two-year registered nurse class. It was the only position open for a student in the hospital. There were six LPNs who invested all they had in me. They trained me well. They taught me to think critically. They poured all they had into me. We are still friends to this day and from time to time, we see each other and catch up.

Leading up to the last semester, my husband and I took our children to

Washington, D.C. We stayed in Arlington, Virginia, because it was cheaper. Every morning we would leave the hotel, find somewhere to park, walk through the gardener's gate at Arlington National Cemetery, and go to the front entrance where we would catch the bus to some museum or point of interest in Washington.

One day, on a particularly tiring day, we lost track of time and caught the last bus back to the cemetery. The crowds were gone and we were tired. Since everyone was worn out, we missed our sign to go back through the gardener's gate. We got turned around. The park had closed with us in there. After rambling around for almost an hour, we came upon the Tomb of the Unknown Soldier. During the summertime they change the guard pretty frequently, so we were thrilled when we saw a live human being marching back and forth guarding the tomb.

We asked him where the gate was. He ignored us. We asked him again. He ignored us again. Finally after asking him several times, we implored him to help us. By this time, the children were out of sorts. Still he didn't answer us. Now I know that the guards have a sacred duty and a sworn trust. They can't talk. But we didn't know that then. Next we saw a jogger on a path and we inquired of the gate. She told us to go to the magnolia tree and make a left. What does a magnolia tree look like? I didn't have a clue back then. So we missed the clue again. We had already been to President Kennedy's tomb with the eternal flame. We saw it again but still didn't know where it was in relationship to the back gate.

Lastly we found the Iwo Jima statue. This was right in front of the gardener's gate. We had finally arrived. Everyone came in and laid down for a nap before dinner. Before we realized it, we had slept the entire night through. We didn't awake until later on the next day. And on that note, we decided to start motoring back to our home in another state.

I did graduate on time. Sometimes during my classes my husband would live with us and other times he wouldn't. The children and I got used to his absences. I had to learn to parent by phone and sleep when I could. We worked rotating shifts so on any given week I would be on a different shift. But we learned to make do. My mother always said you could get used to anything. So I would just work harder to keep things as normal as possible.

I was able to secure a position with the government as a full-time registered nurse. The only position open for a new nurse in the entire hospital was on a cardiac unit. I knew nothing about the heart but of course this didn't stop me. I just figured I would learn as I went along. I was confident that I would do a good job. And learn I did.

God gave me six angels in the bodies of six licensed practical nurses that worked that floor. They poured all of their knowledge into me. A couple had been on that floor for over twenty-five years so they really knew their way around. I am proud to say no one ever expired when I was the charge nurse. I remember one harrowing experience where I was the charge nurse, with one LPN and one student nurse who couldn't even take blood pressures yet.

During this time, I had to parent by phone. He had moved out of the house or been put out of the house for the last time. I was either on first shift or second shift. I was either calling to make sure they got up and out to the school bus on time, or calling to make sure they got home on time and were doing homework, eating dinner, etc. Life was chaotic, but this was nothing new.

He was still working at his middle management position. Even though we didn't live together, we still had an amicable relationship most of the time for the children's sake. One day my car broke down. He took me back and forth to work until I was able to get it fixed. We were able to work around both of our schedules.

During my time in nursing school, I had really become engaged in community work. I volunteered at my children's school. I volunteered in our local community. I was always going to a meeting or sitting on a committee. I wanted to make the world a better place for my children and all the other children.

I believed in the "butterfly" theory. When a butterfly flaps its wings in one hemisphere of this Earth, it has a profound impact on the entire Earth. Everything and everyone is interconnected. Everything that has ever been and everything that will ever be is also connected.

One day, right before my husband left, he and my oldest son were really having a rough time with each other. He treated this son differently and I can only assumed that it was because he was not his biological father. These were some difficult years for all of us. So much screaming, fighting, walking on eggshells, etc. When one person is sick in a home, the entire household is sick.

He always talked to his daughter and from time to time, she would tell me what was going on. I knew who his primary care physician was because he had switched to a new doctor very recently. This doctor did not know his history and my husband neglected to tell him pertinent facts about his history.

Around this time, new medication was being approved for bipolar disorder. That is a diagnosis that my husband had since he was very young. He was selective of the things he told us. All of this came out when our youngest son was sent to a psychologist to be evaluated for a social disorder. The attending psychiatrist wanted to treat our son with a short-term course of a psychotropic medication, but my husband flatly refused. This would haunt the entire family for a lifetime. But at that time, I let my husband have his way. And of course my young son didn't want to have to be on medication either.

The other time I had to leave was when he had purchased two grown poodles. They both were sick with distemper. He didn't have cages to put them in. They had free reign of the house. He didn't clean up after them, didn't see to their needs, etc. He said he brought the dogs for our children. One dog was quite sick and relieved himself every couple of hours. He couldn't control this even though he was supposed to be housebroken. Now, along with three children and a husband to see to, I had two animals.

I asked him repeatedly to get rid of the dogs. He flatly refused. I decided to take matters into my own hands. I rented an apartment one block from our house. It was a very large apartment complex. I took a six-month lease. I took my oldest son with me. On the appointed day, I strapped my son's bed on top of my van. I put the couch inside of the van along with a couple of chairs, some bed sheets, etc., and we moved in.

Before I left, I told my other two children that we would visit often and I showed them how to get to our

new house by using a shortcut or a footpath.
I told them that their father was going to take care of them, send them to school, etc., but they would see their brother and mother often.

The very first day of this arrangement, when I came home, there were my two other children. They said they had come to my house to stay. They said they didn't want to stay with their father. Again, I found myself in the same boat. But this time we were in an apartment, all four of us, and he was living in a whole house, my children's house, with two animals.

After about a month of this arrangement, I convinced him to switch places with me—he moved to the apartment and we moved back home to the house. He saw this opportunity as "freedom." He said he didn't like housework, yard work, etc. So on the "moving day" we made the switch.

The deal was that I would pay our mortgage and he would pay the rent on the apartment. Eventually, I went to the management company and had him sign a new lease as a sublease. Everyone was happy.

Within a couple of months, he was given an eviction notice. He had continued to play his music loud at all times of day and night. He was up and awake all times of day and night. He was a nuisance. They made him pay out the lease and he came back home. And again, things were fine for a while, or we tried to pretend like everything was fine.

The stress was taking its toll on everyone. My husband didn't sleep. He played music very loud all night long. I almost lost my mind. In hindsight, I don't know how those children kept it together as long as they did. And naturally his slide into a manic episode would take its toll at work.

From all I can piece together, this is what finally happened. His job was very stressful. He was getting calls all night from a new program he and his team had written. It had several bugs in it. He was never off the clock. Sometimes they would call at two a.m. and he would have to go in. He wouldn't come home until after dinner the next day.

His response was to take his aggression out on his family. He couldn't tell his boss that job stress was getting to be too much. His salary was increasing with his responsibility. So he had money but no time to spend it.

One day, his first line manager asked him to do something. My husband was sitting at his desk with his feet on his desk reading a newspaper. His response to his boss was: "You do it yourself and leave me alone!"

His manager immediately called security and they escorted my husband to the medical department where he gave up urine for a drug test. He was sent home pending test results. I had already talked to his primary care doctor about his out of control behavior. His doctor told me it was probably a combination of stress and a new medication he had prescribed for my husband. Out of control behavior was a known side effect.

I called my husband and told him what his doctor said about his medication. I urged him to go back to his doctor and get a new medication, one that wouldn't give him these side effects. He flatly refused. He said he loved the way this medication made him feel. He said he didn't require any sleep and he was very creative. Of course, no one could stand him. He was even meaner and nastier than usual.

Now I was trying to see the larger picture. Even when he was out of the house, he still paid child support for his children. My oldest son and I had been on public assistance when I was in school, but his children were never on any type of assistance. But now if he lost his position, I didn't know how I could keep the house, the car, take care of three children, etc., on my salary. It just wasn't enough.

So I went into survival mode. I called his manager and explained my husband's precarious health situation to him. I had his primary care physician working to bring him in to take him off of the medication. Next I called our attorney because his doctor said if things kept going the way they were going, I might have to go through the court system and become his power of attorney. Finally, his doctor said he would be running out of medicine soon and would need a refill. So he put out a precaution to the pharmacy where he got the original prescription filled. They were to call the police if he tried to refill his prescription.

Finally, in the middle of the night, I get a call from the pharmacy. My husband was there but when he saw the police drive up, he left by a different door. So he was still out there, out of medication and in a manic state. Several acquaintances had seen him over the next couple of weeks. They felt sorry for him. He was in a bad way.

Our lawyer and his doctor told me I probably didn't have a choice. I would have to probate him. I had begged his manager not to terminate him until I could find out exactly what was the problem. He agreed to wait for a specific period of time before starting termination procedures.

I went down to our county courthouse armed with evidence from the doctor and on the advice of our attorney. I filed the necessary papers. He was picked up and taken to our local county psychiatric hospital. After being held for seventy-two hours for an evaluation, he was released to a private hospital where he would get the care he needed.

It just so happened that my sister's significant other worked in intake at our county psych hospital. He knew my husband very well and was on duty when my husband was brought into the hospital by our local police department. No one in my family knew the "hell " my children and I had been living in. And of course, everyone accused me of being one of the most despicable human beings that ever lived for doing *that* to my husband.

After he was evaluated, I had to go back to court and give testimony why I thought he was a danger to himself and others. I talked about the medicine and his decline after he took the medicine. The doctor defended his use of the medicine because my husband didn't tell the doctor he had a previous diagnosis of bipolar disorder. The doctor said he never would have ordered that particular medication in light of that previous diagnosis.

Once I got my husband settled in a private hospital, I would visit everyday. He seemed glad for the company. He was put on a different psychotropic drug. After a couple of weeks of therapy, he was released and told to go to outpatient counseling, which he did. That doctor determined that it was probably best if my husband filed for Social Security disability. He never went back to work at that position or for that company again.

One Saturday, while I was getting the children ready for our weekend activities, we heard a commotion on our front lawn. During those years, all of the children played t-ball during the summer months. Our typical Saturdays consisted of early morning baths and breakfast then out the door for all day activities. This particular Saturday started out as any typical Saturday morning. When I opened our front door, there was a man planting a "For Sale" sign on our front yard. He told me he was a realtor who was hired by my husband to sell the house. My husband had not discussed this with me. In fact, he hadn't said one word to me about moving. He knew the children and I loved that house. Children had their own room. There was a large in ground pool in the back that offered endless hours of fun for everyone.

When I asked the realtor about the sign selling the house, he said my husband had entered into contract with his company and had hired them to sell the house. My husband didn't need the money to live on, but we needed the house to live in.

My children were quite upset at the notion of moving. I tried to act like everything was okay, but on the inside it seemed like my world was coming apart. And to make matters worse, I was working night shift and would try to sleep during the day. But the realtor insisted on showing the house during the day with me in bed trying to sleep. Several clients came through and eventually a contract was made on our house.

The realtor called and asked if he could come over the next day to get my signature on the contract. The prospective clients were anxious to get a loan so they could close soon. I agreed to see the realtor the following day. Wouldn't you know it, the following day was a Saturday and that meant everyone was home. My children sat at my feet and listened intently as the realtor went over the standard contract with me.

Before I could say anything, my children began to cry. They asked me: "Mommy, if we have to move, where will we live?" I didn't have an answer for them. I assured them that we would find somewhere to live where we all would be together. That wasn't good enough for them. They told me they didn't want to leave their house, their neighborhood and their friends. They asked why their daddy would do this to us? I told them I didn't know. Finally, I told the realtor that I would not sign the contract.

The real estate agent became angry with me and told me I couldn't stop my husband from selling it since my name was not on the deed. That much was true. But he didn't know what I had just heard. While the children were crying, I was praying and saying along with the realtor that I couldn't keep the house. I couldn't pay the mortgage, the taxes and insurance; buy food, clothes, etc., not on my salary. Then I heard a still small voice say to my heart: "No, you can't keep it, but I can." "Trust and believe." It has not been an easy journey, but I am still in that house over 20 years later. God is faithful!

Now I don't mean to say that my husband was the worst person in the world. I believe I brought out the worst in him as he brought out the worst in me.

We eventually tried to build new lives for ourselves without each other. He met a very nice young lady and I have seen her over the years. We are on speaking terms. This lady was the one he asked me for a divorce over. He said he wanted to marry her. When he first asked me for a divorce, I was adamant about not giving him one. Over the years I mellowed. I eventually told him he could have a divorce anytime he wanted one. All he had to do was bring me the papers and I would sign them.

I have met some interesting men during my separation. We lived our lives as if we were both single.

My girlfriend was working as a nurse several years after my husband and I had split. She met a gentleman whom she believed would be a good fit for me. So one day she asked if she could give him my number and I agreed.

We met at the movies. I noticed immediately that he had a very thick accent. He was from "the islands." We would date for the next five or six years. Eventually he would get a key to my house. Every now and then I could get him to make island food. I loved his cooking. He had a daughter who was my daughter's age and lived near my youngest sister. Our families became good friends.

My husband had a habit of coming to my house uninvited if he heard I had someone new in my life. He would try to intimidate the other party. This gentleman was hard to intimidate since he outweighed my husband by about 30 pounds. Plus he was taller than my husband. My husband went to college on a football scholarship and had maintained his weight and his physique all through the years. He was fastidious about his exercise regime. He lived to go to the gym and exercise. Anyway, this gentleman didn't scare easy.

Have you ever met someone who is the nicest person you have ever met but they don't want anything in life? That's how this gentleman was. I couldn't get him to go to school and finish his GED. He didn't want to learn a trade. He didn't want to improve his English. As far as I could tell, he was happy sitting around watching Kung Fu movies all the time. He has never cut the grass, trimmed the hedges or taken out the garbage without being asked. And then he complained all the time he was doing it. This just wouldn't work for me and after five or six years or coaxing, cajoling and trying to instill some sort of "hustle" in him, it was time to cut my losses and move on.

But we still remain very good friends to this day. We email each other and go out to eat periodically. He reconciled with his wife and they have three grandchildren.

I eventually met another man that I thought I wanted to marry, but that never happened either. I met a man from Africa who was on his way up the political ladder. We kept in touch over many years. He traveled extensively outside of his home country. One day he asked me if I had ever traveled outside of the USA, I had to tell him no. He suggested to me that if I ever got to chance to do some international travel to please take that opportunity. He said travel broadened you as a person. I promised him I would. And life went on.

The very next year I received a letter from this gentleman. It was written in flawless English. He was inquiring about my family and I. He told me he and his wife just had a brand new baby boy after two girls. All were healthy and doing fine.

The next year, I got a package, from him, which contained a handmade African dress. It was a beautiful blue with gold stitching and piping. I thanked him for it by return letter. We continue to talk either by letter or telephone. One day he asked me what my email was and I told him. Then our conversations picked up because we began to do them by email.

One day after many years of communication, he stopped by my hometown on his way to his home. He had been to Brazil and since he was changing planes about five hours from my home, he decided to do a holiday with me. His timing could not have been more off. Also this would be the first time I had seen him in many years.

I picked him up at the airport and brought him to my house. By this time, the children were grown and only coming in sporadically. It was difficult to have someone in my home that had different eating and sleeping habits than I had, but we managed.

And as usual my husband showed up. It was a beautiful spring day. I had the front door opened because my houseguest loved sitting and eating on the front porch. That is what he did in his country. Nobody stays in the house. You get up in the morning and get ready for the day. You take all of your meals outdoors with others. It is truly the definition of "communal" eating.

My husband walked right in the unlocked screen door and introduced himself as my husband. Luckily I had told this man everything about us. I heard them downstairs talking as I was upstairs. I came downstairs immediately and asked my husband what did he want? He said he wanted to meet this gentleman since he heard he was in town for a few days. Of course one of the children had told their father about this man.

Well my husband's visit had the desired effect. My houseguest felt like he should leave since my husband had said I was still his wife and that was still his house. I guess technically he was correct. But I convinced him not to leave.

We had wonderful conversations on how we could collaborate together. I told him of my desire to eventually visit Africa. He told me he would host me and anyone else I wanted to come to Africa with me. He had good relationship with my children. I suspect they like him because he was from a foreign country and could enlighten them about a foreign culture.

Over the years we kept in touch. I watched his rise to the highest pinnacles of politics in his country. And I always promised him that one of those days I would visit. And eventually I did.

By this time my husband and I were truly living separate lives. When my oldest graduated from high school my husband came to the graduation and then back to my house for a small reception. We were now on amicable terms.

And sometimes I didn't see him for months on end. But I would inquire of him with our daughter and son who kept up with him.

CHAPTER 5

Ascension

By this time I had hit rock bottom. I graduated on time with my nursing degree and went to work as a nurse. I was struggling everyday. I worked as a cardiac nurse. I would cry before I went to work and cry when I came home from work. I was miserable. To say I was depressed is not enough. I finally quit my job and took a job through an agency hoping this would help. I was sent to many different places as an agency nurse. I thought a change of scenery might help, but it didn't.

I did correctional medicine, long-term care. I did flu shots and school nursing. I became a CPR instructor and a trainer for our county Department of Jobs and Family Services. With this, I did training of daycare/childcare workers, which I still do. I did pediatric nursing, which is where I was when I "crashed and burned."

The time came when I could no longer hurt the way I was hurting. So I made up my mind to leave this mean and cruel world. Whenever anyone would ask me when my birthday was, I would tell them a different day than my actual birthday. I would tell them the day I had planned to go to Heaven.

I was hearing voices. They would murmur such sweet things to me. They would soothe me with words of comfort, telling me I didn't have to endure this pain and hardship any longer. They would tell me that I was unlovable and everyone including myself would be better off without me. I would hear the voices all times of day or night. And it came a time when I believed these caring voices. Now I know that they were not the right voices to be listening to.

So on the prescribed day, my new birthday, I went to work as usual. I took care of my four-month-old charge all the while trying to decide what would be a good time for me to go to Heaven. Should I leave immediately when I got to work? Should I work a few hours then kill myself or should I wait until the end of my shift and then take my life? I just couldn't make up my mind.

But I still heard the voices—and they were insistent. They were trying to reason with me about what difference did time make? Maybe I should do it sooner rather than waiting for later. That sounded like a good plan to me.

And as I went about my duties taking care of my case, I heard a strange new voice. It was a singular voice. It was calm and even. It told me to call someone immediately and tell that person I was sick and I needed to go to the hospital.

Now this voice was truly different from the other voices I had been hearing. This voice seemed to genuinely care about me. This voice sounded like it wanted a different outcome than the one I had planned. You see, my reasoning was so warped that I believed the young child should go to Heaven with me. She shouldn't be left here to experience all the bad things on this Earth. I also believed my own children would be better off without me. They would be taken care of by my family. They would have great lives without me.

But this one voice just kept repeating, in a nice even tone, to call someone and tell them to take me to the hospital. Something told me I should trust this voice over all the other ones that I was hearing. I decided to comply.

Now who do you think I called? That's right! My husband. He immediately came and took me to our large teaching hospital. I was evaluated by emergency psychological services. Because I was clearly suicidal and possibly homicidal, I was immediately admitted and placed on suicide watch. My husband walked me upstairs to my room and sat with me as I got settled in. He promised to go by the house, to talk to our children about my condition.

One of the first orders of business when you are on suicide watch is to sign a paper saying you will not kill yourself during this hospitalization. I guess this exempts them from any liability. At any rate, I signed the papers and stayed in my room until I was given permission to come out. I decided as always to be a compliant patient.

I was allowed to come out to eat but since I didn't know anyone, I didn't do a lot of socializing. This hospitalization just seemed to start out differently than the first two. With the other ones, I was not suicidal. I had actually wanted to live. With this one I did not.

Finally nighttime arrived and I was told to try to get some sleep, even though there would be a nurses coming in to check on me every hour as was protocol for those on "suicide watch." After the nurse had checked on me for about four hours and I had not fallen asleep at all, he called the doctor and got an order for a sleeping pill. I took the pill and still I was unable to sleep.

In the very early morning hours, I must have fallen asleep because I became aware of someone tapping me on my outer hip as I was lying on my side. I rolled over to see who wanted to talk to me.

My room was dark. The door was open and there was an electric exit sign right across from my door. Plus my room was right next to the nursing station and there was a light on in that office.

I could not see my visitor clearly but I could make out some features. He was in his middle 40s. He had black hair with copper skin. He had on a beautiful royal blue suit. He also had on a white button down shirt with a royal blue and black tie. He was sitting on the side of my bed.

When He looked at me it was like he was looking right into the heart of me. There was no pretense on either of our parts. And when He looked at me, I immediately started to cry. I don't mean sniffles, nice girly-girl polite sobs. I mean honest to goodness, have yourself a good cry sobs. I was retching from deep within my soul. I was crying from a place that had never been opened before. He opened me up and exposed what I had hidden from the world. I lay there bare and vulnerable.

Finally, when I could compose myself, He asked me if I knew who He was, and I said yes. Then He asked me if I knew why I was in the hospital, and I said yes again. This time He told me no, I didn't know why I was there. Again I disagreed and I told Him I knew exactly why I was in the hospital and I went on to tell Him that I was suicidal. Finally He told me that I was in the hospital because I was trying to handle life all by myself.

He told me He was there to make an agreement with me. He asked me if I would hand control of my life over to Him. And He told me to think about my answer. Then He said if I didn't like that way He was handling my life, I could ask Him for it back and He would give it back to me.

Then He asked me for my decision. I agreed to give Him control of my life, right then and right there. He said all right and to go back and try to get some sleep. Then He walked out of my room.

I must have fallen asleep because the next thing I know, I was being awakened by a nurse for morning meds. Then I was told to get dressed so I could go out to breakfast. After that I had to meet with the psychiatrist, the social worker for one-on-one therapy, and then I would have group therapy.

Again I did what I was told. This was still the same nurse whom I had seen several times the previous night. I asked him about the doctor who came to visit me the previous night.

He denied that anyone other than himself had come into my room the entire shift. He said no doctor had come on the floor during the entire shift last night. He even went so far as to suggest that I was still hallucinating when I spoke of the man in the suit who came to see me and talked with me the previous night. After a while, I could tell that I was getting nowhere with him and I didn't want him to put anything negative in my chart. They thought I would probably only be in the hospital for one week, and I didn't want that to change based on some allegations or misunderstandings with the staff.

Now I can't tell you that my life changed overnight, but I can tell you that it did change. I was discharged after one week and went to outpatient therapy. I never went back to that job, but I didn't lose my nursing license either.

I was hospitalized and had a Visitor who changed my life completely. From that experience and my history, I was put on Social Security disability. But I believed I was still young enough to work. Plus, I still had two children at home.

One day, a couple of years later, my phone rang. It was my BFF No. 1. She said another classmate of ours had called her and asked if she was interested in a part-time position at this classmate's church. My friend said that she would come to the interview but she doubted it very seriously. My BFF number 1 said she had children at home and she still needed benefits.

This position was for a Parish Nurse. When my BFF number 1 asked me if I was interested in the position, my first question was: "What is a parish nurse?" And my next statement was: "I can't be a parish nurse because I am not Catholic." She still insisted that I come along to the interview just in case it was something of interest.

I met my BFF at a hospice, which is where the interview was to take place. The owner of the hospice was doing the interview. He was looking for someone to go into a large African American church as a parish nurse. His company paid a stipend to cover expenses for this part-time position. It did not pay any benefits or salary. My BFF had to flatly turn it down. He got the idea from the Lutheran Church where he was a deacon and where the parish nurse movement was growing.

The owner had paid an LPN on his staff to do the groundwork for the position. The LPN couldn't take the position because you had to be an RN to work independently as a parish nurse. His reasoning for starting this program was he was looking to service African American patients. He had never had a black parish nurse in their five years of operation of that hospice.

A woman who had left the nunnery had taken the position for one year. She was coming upon her 65th birthday when she could retire. She had met a man in Florida and she wanted to get married and move to Florida and live out the rest of her days there with him.

I thought it was wonderful. This lady who had been a nun for over forty years had found love and was willing to risk everything for love. Also, I had heard a lot about the church where I would be working. I knew some members who went to that church and they spoke very highly of the pastor, his wife and the entire worship experience there.

So with little hesitation, I agreed to take this part-time position with no salary, no benefits and just a stipend to cover expenses. Plus I had an office at the hospice with use of their office equipment.

The nun was leaving in two weeks, so she had that much time to train me. She gave me a small brown box with her resources in it. Our first stop would be to the church on Sunday to introduce me to the Pastor. She and I sat together. And when service was over, she pulled his robe as he passed by and pointed to me. He bowed his head as if to say I understand. This is our new Parish Nurse.

I went on hospital visits and home visits with her. We went to nursing homes and trainings. She showed me where to park for free at the hospitals and where to eat for reduced prices. She took me to large and small not-for-profits and introduced me as her replacement. She showed me where to get all kinds of resources. She told me that when I worked as a parish nurse, I was part of the clergy team of that congregation.

And finally we had to say goodbye. I kept in touch with her over the next several months. Unfortunately her brother became ill in another part of the country. She elected to go and take care of him. She never did get married. As far as I know, she is still taking care of her brother.

When I started as parish nurse, I had to explain it to everyone I met. It was so new that most people had never heard of it. In fact, I hadn't heard of it until I went to the interview. An offshoot of it is called "Health Ministries."

I told you I knew several people at the congregation where I went to work. One of them was my first husband, my eldest son's father. He was a deacon there. I never told anyone about our prior marriage, but he told everyone. This congregation welcomed me with open arms. It also helped that my pastor was a good friend of the pastor of the church where I was working. I would split my time on Sundays between my home church and my work church.

This church was known to be on the forefront of civic and social issues. The pastor and his wife invested all they had into me. He would allow me to accompany him to meetings and social functions. He always introduced me as the nurse who worked at his church.

About one year after I took the position, the announcement was put in the church bulletin that the church was going to Israel and Egypt the following year. Oh, how my heart "burned" to be able to go to these places. So when the initial meeting was set, I made up my mind to be there.

This trip would be a dream come true for me. But the price was more than I could afford. But I still put my name on the list as someone who would be going. We had one year to raise the money. And not only would I have to come up with the money to go, I would have to come up with childcare as well.

I kept right on making every meeting. Eventually at one of the meetings, I met my potential roommate. We got along wonderfully. I was excited.

I called the children's father and told him of this wonderful opportunity. He told me he would handle childcare. He said he could make sure the children came home, were fed and put to bed. By this time, we were no longer fighting. He had found someone he was seriously interested in.

He had asked me for a divorce and by this time, I had agreed to it. I had told him to just bring the papers by my house and I would sign them. He was happy after all this time of separation.

As the final meeting approached, I was excited. I had everything in order. I had a passport, luggage packed and the house in order. I had even managed to pay all of the money on time.

Two days before departure, I got a call from the children's father. He informed me that he had changed his mind and he would not be offering childcare. He said I would just have to forfeit my airfare and hotel. His only explanation was that he just didn't feel like being bothered.

Again, I felt blindsided. How could I have trusted him yet again? Did I have some type of masochistic wish? I must love being hurt by this man! It never failed, whenever I depended on him, he never came through. He didn't come though for his children either. It is like he felt no responsibility for their happiness. And Heaven forbid that I would find some happiness along the way. He was doing everything he could to sabotage my happiness.

So I did the only thing I could do. I called the pastor and told him I couldn't go because my childcare arrangements had just fallen through. This pastor told me to try to make the final meeting anyway. He said we would pray over the situation and see what happened.

I came to the meeting and sat in the back. I was very quiet and subdued. I heard them making plans, talking about all the sights, sounds, smells and new adventures they would experience. My heart was so heavy.

We would first fly to New York where we would board an El Air flight to Tel Aviv, Israel. After we did the Holy Land tour, we would come across the Golan Heights by vehicle, get on a barge at the mouth of the Nile River and float downstream. Eventually, we would disembark in Cairo, Egypt. Then we would visit the Pyramids, the Sphinx and other sites of antiquity.

I had to accept my lot in life was not to experience any of them. They were even planning on filming everything. Everyone was asked to bring their Bible as we would be following Matthew and Luke's gospel very closely.

After the meeting, the pastor asked about my plans. I was very candid about my situation. I had saved some money for souvenirs but I didn't go to the bank to get any traveler's checks since I was not going. That was on a Saturday and our plane would leave in two days, on a Monday morning at nine-thirty. I would carry on in my home and hometown while the rest of our team went on the vacation of a lifetime.

This pastor was the president of a large pastoral group in our hometown. He said if I still wanted to go, they would put out my need over all the pulpits the following day, which was a Sunday, to everyone who was a member.

I just want to stop right here and say: "God is faithful!" Several people stepped forward and said they would do it. I had to trust my instinct because I had never seen any of them before. I finally settled on a woman who had one child who went to the same school district as my children. She would pick up her child and they would spend the night at my house. There was plenty of food in the refrigerator and I gave her a few dollars for incidentals. I told her if she needed anything else, to call my family and they would give it to her and I would pay them back when I got back.

I caught a ride to our boarding place with some other travelers. I had to stop at the ATM on my way to catch our bus. I was limited in what I could take out. Besides, I didn't have very much in there in the first place. But I got what I could and trusted God that He would meet my needs. And He did.

Finally after many hours waiting in the airport and after finally getting through security, we were airborne. I was on the biggest plane that I had ever seen. It was a 747. Since then I have been on a 777 and A130 Airbuses, but I had never been out of the States before. I had never flown over an ocean for sure.

The pastor had everyone sit with their roommate so we could really get to know each other. He didn't want any tensions spoiling this trip. After we had eaten a sumptuous meal, we settled back for a long oceanic crossing, and then on to Israel.

I encountered several obstacles that I had to overcome if I was to survive this trip. First, we finally discovered how to view where we were in relationship to a world map and our destination. I really got a feeling for how much ocean was out there. And because I knew a lot about the continent of Africa, I knew there were mountains in the ocean that were taller than Mount Kilimanjaro, which is the tallest mountain in Africa.

Next, I had never felt turbulence like that before. Funny thing is, the cabin attendants never stopped working. It seemed like the turbulence didn't affect them. But it affected my roommate and me a lot. In fact, every time we encountered some turbulence, we would stop talking, bow our heads and begin to pray.

Finally, it came a time when were smack dab over the middle of the Atlantic Ocean. We were just as far from New York as we were from London, England. We reasoned that if we got in trouble and went down, there were no ships coming to rescue us. There were no helicopters that could fly out that far or any other plane that could land on the water to get us. We would really be on our own. Besides there were fish in the ocean that ate meat and we would look like dinner to them.

And on top of everything else, we hit a particularly bad bit of turbulence. Naturally, we stopped talking and went to our "fall back" positions, which was talking with God. Now I don't know what, if anything, He said to anyone else. But He spoke to my heart just as plain as day. He said: "Marsha, it is only the wind. I have given you authority over the wind. If you don't like the wind then you need to tell it to settle down."

Now imagine the God of the Universe would take time to calm my fears? He gave me a life lesson in those few sentences. Immediately but hesitantly I decided to do what He said do. Very shakily, I told the wind that I didn't like it to shake the plane. I told the wind that the plane shaking frightened me and it would have to settle down. I told the wind that by the authority of Jesus it would have to do what I told it to do. I said all of this under my breath.

And low and behold, that big jumbo jet, with six hundred people on it, leveled out like a babe taking a nap. I thought to myself, now we are really onto something now. This is amazing. I was beginning to understand authority and dominion through this demonstration.

I—like Mary, the mother of Jesus—treasured these things in my heart as we finally arrived in Tel Aviv, Israel, and went to our hotel. We checked in and my roommate and I stayed up most of the night talking. We were so excited that we couldn't sleep.

There were so many wonders to behold. Our tour guide took us on the Christian tour. Wherever we went, our pastor would have us read about that place from our Bible. It was thrilling. I was in the land where Jesus walked. We hit the highlights of His life here on Earth. I even brought home a clipping from the six trees that are still standing in the Garden of Gethsemane after two thousand years. Oh, if those trees could talk!

We went to The Mount of Beatitudes. It was a beautiful place. It was early spring when we arrived. The flowers were in bloom. The birds were singing. And you could look down the mountainside onto the Sea of Galilee. I thought it was the most beautiful place on this Earth.

I sat on a bench all by myself to admire the scenery and talk to God. I told Him how beautiful I thought that spot on Earth was. And again, He spoke to me. First He told me He knew I would love that place when I finally saw it. Then He told me that before he scooped out the seabed, He thought of me. He said He did it because He loved me. He told me He loved me with every drop of water in the Sea of Galilee. He said He loved me with every blade of grass on that hillside and with every song that every bird was singing. That was how much He loved me!

Wow, by this time, tears are streaming down my face. At first when He started talking I had looked around to see if I could see Him. Then I realized that He was speaking directly to my heart and not to my ears. So I had closed my eyes and bowed my head.

Then all of a sudden I heard my roommate and the pastor's wife called my name. I was immediately upset because they were intruders into my special time with Jesus. And

I knew I wouldn't be able to keep that connection to Him with them asking me questions. I didn't want to have to answer any questions about why was I crying, etc.

But at last I did answer, but I answered in the form of my own questions such as: "Did you see Him?" or "Did you hear Him?" They wanted to know whom I was talking about because I was sitting on the bench by myself? I kept quizzing them about seeing or hearing anyone. They flatly denied seeing or hearing anyone special other than the hum or snatches of other conversations. So I didn't press the issue any more and neither did they.

But that evening I told my roommate all about what happened to me. She was very excited. She said she wished she could have an encounter like that. She realized it was nothing I did that precipitated the encounter. It was really on Jesus' part.

On one of our last days in Israel, we went to the Tomb. I just want to tell you, I looked inside. It really is empty. He got up! The Tomb is empty! He is risen!

The day came for us to say goodbye to Israel and board a bus, which took us across the Golan Heights to the mouth of the Nile River. We boarded a barge and floated down the Nile. Eventually we got off the barge in Cairo, Egypt.

As I told you, I was twelve years old when I stated I wanted to go to Egypt. And here I had finally arrived. Of course one of our first stops was a visit to the Great Pyramids of Giza. There we visited the Sphinx where only I, out of several hundred people, knew the riddle of the Sphinx. Egypt is known for its fabric so we visited a couple of textile mills and a carpet-making warehouse. We ate the local cuisine and sampled many epicurean delights.

After several days in Egypt, we boarded a plane that would take us back to New York City. As we waited on the tarmac, I fell asleep.

My roommate who was still sitting next to me on the return trip remarked at how much I had changed during the trip. I told her that I didn't think I had changed at all, but she kept insisting that I had. I left her to her opinion and really didn't give it anymore thought until later on in life.

I realized that you can't have an encounter with an eternal being and not be changed. Of course, I was changed for the better. This was just another example of Him having control of my life.

After working this position for about three years, the funding source dried up. The pastor and his wife called me into the office and told me the church's budget just couldn't handle a stipend much less a salary. So I left but we still remain good friends. And when my eldest son is in town, he always visits his father's church and I go with him.

Have you ever heard of those serendipity moments? I remember one real well. I had read in a local magazine that an organization was looking for nominees for recognition in certain categories. And one category was Medicine/Health.

A couple of years before this, I had been selected as The Most Distinguished Alumni of my junior college. I have come to appreciate this honor more and more as I have gotten older. I always say that it is a working position because I represent them wherever I go and I make them look good. But as the college has grown and become more regional, the truth is, they make me look good.

So when I saw the nomination I figured I would get my BFF number 1 to write another recommendation for me. When I asked her, she agreed. Then because I was one of the finalists, I was told that I would be invited to the awards ceremony where the winner would be announced. I could also bring a guest. We both loved to eat upscale food so we relished the opportunity just to come to the pre-party and enjoy dinner by the bite.

Times were still hard as I was now on Social Security disability, which is a lot less than a regular salary. I needed a formal dress for this occasion and I didn't have one to my name. So I began to scour second-hand stores. I also had to have a picture taken to go into the souvenir brochure. Luckily, the organization paid for a professional photo. I pulled an old pants suit out of the closet, ironed it up really good and went to the photo shoot. While there, I met the other finalists in all of the categories.

I met my competition. One was an eye doctor who had been in practice for thirty-seven years. Another was a psychologist who had a tremendous practice. The other contestant was a social worker who had started the first African American breast cancer support group. And then there was me, the first parish nurse in our city.

My youngest sister decided she would come and support me. And lo and behold, my older sister on my mother's side flew in for the occasion. She said she wanted to support me as well. Everyone thought it was a tremendous honor just to be nominated and so did I. So I was content just to enjoy the festivities of the evening.

When we arrived, we were shown into a private dining room where we ate a sumptuous meal. We were also given a copy of the brochure. I was so excited to just get all dressed up with my BFF No. 1, we didn't pay very much attention to the brochure. I didn't see there was a full-page ad congratulating me. I didn't think too much about it.

This was as big as it gets in my mid-sized Midwestern city. This was akin to the Oscars. And we were finally led upstairs and seated. By then my two sisters had arrived and were seated beside me. Then the lights went down and the music started.

This awards ceremony took place every year and it was a highly anticipated event. The suspense was enough to generate numerous conversations and speculations. I didn't have to speculate on my category. I was up against three heavy hitters, so my chance of winning was a long shot at best.

And finally the category of Medicine/Health came up. They showed each picture and told why the person was a finalist. I heard my name, saw my picture while they talked of my accolades.

I was nominated because I was using faith communities to get the word out about health issues. Very early in my career as a parish nurse, I had learned that faith communities were trusted institutions. They are the only institutions that interacted with you from birth to death. And if the leader says, "Today we will have our blood pressure taken," you best believe the entire faith community will try to comply. I had also learned a lot of large not-for-profit, disease-oriented organizations had faith-based programs. But they were looking for someone with cultural competency to offer the programs. I became the go-to person for these programs.

I was drawn out of my reverie by the emcee saying: "And the winner is…Marsha D. Thomas!" I just sat there stunned. I felt like I was underwater, like I was drowning. I couldn't take a breath much less come to the podium to receive my award.

BFF No. 1 and my two sisters were congratulating me. And then the searchlights began to go back and forth over the finalists and I heard my name repeated several times. They were asking for me to please come to the stage and accept my award.

I finally made it to stage. My knees were shaking so badly that I could only get to the nearest podium and collapse there. I grabbed the podium to steady myself. I asked the emcees if I could just stand there and they said yes.

After I received my award, I was required to give a brief speech. And the first words I could think of were:

"To God Be The Glory For The Things That He Has Done." Oh, what a momentous occasion that was. I made my way back to my seat after thanking the committee, my parents, my family and friends. My knees still felt like jello, but I gingerly walked down from the podium and back to my seat while the spotlight stayed on me.

It was an incredible night to say the least. It was also the start of something fantastic. When I got home that night, my daughter told me that she knew that I had won. I asked her how she knew that? She said it was because she saw it on the news, on the TV.

All of this happened on a Saturday night. On that following Monday I had to show up for a photo shoot for all of the winners. That shoot became part of a permanent exhibit at our Arts Center, which is part of our Museum Center. This center is housed in our century old Union Terminal. During the terminal's heyday, it was used as our central railroad depot. Upwards of thirty trains would leave there everyday. In fact this is the same terminal that my mother and my father used to escape the segregated South and Jim Crow. It was also the same terminal that I traveled to with my mother as a newborn.

As a parish nurse, I had the opportunity to meet some incredible people. These people were changing the health scene in our city one person at a time. One such person, Ms. Judith Warren, was at the awards ceremony. So it was no surprise to me when I ran into her at another community meeting a few months later. She asked me two questions that would impact me significantly over the life of my career: (1) Was I still doing parish nursing? Yes. (2) Was I still doing it for free? Again, the answer was yes. She suggested that we sit down and have a conversation. She believed she was in a position to help me and I was in a position to help others.

Eventually we did have a conversation. She told me that she worked for a large funder who was looking for innovative programs to fund. Parish nursing was on their radar. I was in a unique position since I was a lifelong member of a large church. I already had great relationships with pastors, priests, rabbis, congregations and community stakeholders in our city. And I had a large network of community resources that supported me in my efforts.

The result of our meetings and eventually collaboration were four part-time Parish Nurse programs strategically placed in our deteriorating inner city. I was to be the program manager since I had the expertise. And all of this came with a salary for each position!

Amazing how many organizations came looking for me when word got out that I was looking for a fiduciary organization. I finally chose one based on prior relationship and a shared history.

Before I chose this organization, I did a missionary trip to Kenya in East Africa. Nothing could prepare you for abject poverty. But nothing could also prepare you for the beauty of the people, the land and the animals.

I had the opportunity to travel with a Christian organization. At our last planning meeting we were told that if we felt the need to pray for anyone, to stop what we were doing if possible and pray mightily for that person. I was the triage nurse. We saw seventeen hundred people over four days. Which meant I saw seventeen hundred people over four days. I got the opportunity to see every person who came to our clinic.

Clinics in developing countries are not like our clinics in this country. First off, there is no way to efficiently get the word out except word of mouth. So on the first day, you may have a small turnout, but as word spreads, more and more people will show up. So each day, the groundswell is larger and larger. Even though you might set a certain cut off period, the patients are the ones who really dictate when you get done that day.

On my third day there, I was writing in a chart at my table and I heard the scraping of chairs and the moving of furniture. I looked up and I saw a woman walking to my table. She was very weak and emaciated. I knew right away she had the "wasting" disease. In American we call it AIDS. Nobody wanted to get close to her. We didn't know a lot about it back then. Someone eventually took her to the main hospital, Kenyatta, because our makeshift clinic was not equipped to handle those major emergencies.

My heart was immediately touched and I was reminded of a Scripture: "There but for the grace of God go I." I was acutely aware that she was no different than I was. She was probably a wife, a mother, a sister, a daughter. She had the same wants and needs I did. She was born in a country that did not have the resources to care for its most vulnerable citizens. Women and children tended to be marginalized, ostracized and disenfranchised in those patriarchal societies.

Again God revealed Himself in the slums of Nairobi, Kenya. After that, we caught a small charter plane and flew out over the Riff Valley into Mara Mara Game Preserve and the Serengeti Game Preserve. I saw wild animals doing what they had been doing since the beginning of time. Since experiencing that, I have never been able to set foot into a zoo again. I just can't bear to see creatures that were meant to roam free, caged up and begging for scraps of food. That is not what God intended.

During that trip I began to feel the stirrings of a "burden" for women and children. I was especially aware of what drives human trafficking. I have seen it everywhere I go. In America, it is abuse and domestic violence that leads children to run away and end up being trafficked. In developing countries, it is poverty.

One of the doctors I traveled with had just started a nonprofit agency to impact the inner city. That organization became the fiduciary agent for our Parish Nurse Program. The program went under after a couple of years but this doctor and I still have a wonderful working relationship.

Over the next few years, I would come into contact and relationships with many different denominations. I saw more similarities and differences. They all wanted the same thing—good health, meaningful vocations and joyful avocations. I went on to run faith-based initiatives for large not-for-profits. I became the "nurse who worked in churches." I had one foot in the health care arena and one foot in the faith arena. I blended the two.

My wanderlust has always been in high gear. And God has always been faithful. I got to do some incredible things through parish nursing. I brought a program to our city called The Black Church Week of Prayer for the Healing of AIDS. This was a program of an organization called: The Balm in Gilead. They flew me to New Jersey, all expenses paid for the training. When the group came back, we organized a day of healing to educate faith communities. There was so much misconception and stigma out there. People who were at the end of their lives and desperately needed a lifeline from their faith communities were denied this healing because of the nature of this disease.

There came a time when I reviewed my career as a parish nurse and realized I had worked every model of parish nursing known. I had been faith based, institutional based. I had been paid and a volunteer. I had been full time and I had been part time. These models gave me the opportunity to present three times at the annual conference given by the International Parish Nurse Resource Center, first in Chicago and then in St. Louis.

I have given so many talks and so many speeches that I have lost count. And I still continue to work with faith communities on faith-based initiatives. I am continually amazed at how God can take someone like me and use me in the ways that He has.

I like to think that I have made a difference in everyone's life He has allowed me to touch. I am a firm believer that no one comes into our lives by accident. It is all preordained. And everyone who comes into my life brings me a gift. It is up to me to find the gift. Most of the time it is like peeling away the layers of an onion. It is painful when you are doing it, but the end results are amazing.

And along the way, He has allowed me to have some incredible experiences. I told you that I have spoken to our trade group three times. I have attended the conference more times than that. One of the times I was going to Chicago for the conference, I had to decide if I wanted to fly or drive. I had some relatives in Chicago and I had planned on seeing them when I was there. I made the decision late to drive. It was a few days before the conference when I decided to call and order a rental car.

A couple of days before I was due to leave, 9/11 hit. No planes were flying. All modes of transportation were difficult to impossible to arrange. I told my pastor that I just didn't think I should go and he asked why wouldn't I go? So I called to reconfirm my car rental. Wouldn't you know that it was still a go and they still had a car for me? In fact I got an upgrade for free. I went and had a wonderful time. Truly the crowd was small—only those who could drive from a few states came. Usually we had people there from all over the world.

I also met a woman through my work in the AIDS arena who led me to the largest missionary conference in the USA. I try to go each year. One year Ebola struck terror in the hearts of people working outside of the U.S. One American doctor in particular made headlines because he contracted the disease. He was sent back here to the States where he was treated and cured.

That year, he was our keynote speaker. He talked each morning on how he first treated people with Ebola and then how he contracted the disease. A colleague of his became his primary care doctor in West Africa. She helped maintain his life until he could be airlifted back to the States. She came to the conference as well and told about his harrowing journey with that deadly disease. She talked about not having anything to fight that disease with and how each day was touch and go, not knowing what the outcome would be.

On the final day of the conference, his admonition was to follow where your heart was leading. He said that he was on his way back to the area that was disease ridden, but he was convinced that is where God wanted him. His wife stood beside him and spoke those very same words. What a testimony!

One day I had a vision. I saw a door that I had never seen before. It had a nameplate on it. The nameplate had my name and credentials on it. God impressed upon me that He was sending me somewhere else to work. I began to search job sites on the Internet looking for opportunities. Eventually I found one in San Francisco. The hospital system flew me out for a three-day interview.

At the end of the three days, I accepted the position. I was hesitant because it was so far away from my home. But I was learning to trust God. A couple of weeks after I returned home, I got a called from the woman I would report to directly. She asked if I would be terribly upset if they hired someone local. (We had parity in credentials and education, but she knew the prevailing systems in that area.) I said of course not. Secretly I was happy for them and her. Northern California is expensive and the temperature dips down at night. Plus it is a great distance from my home in the Midwest.

Again I began to search websites for opportunities. I found one in Dallas, Texas. I couldn't see if the position had been filled or not so I picked up the phone and called them. They told me that it had not been filled and would I like to apply? I told them I would, so I forwarded them an application and my resume.

They flew me out for an interview. It was with nine women initially. Then I went and spoke with the pastor. Lastly I spoke with the lay pastor to whom I would be reporting. Even though they tried to make sure we didn't have a conversation with each other, it was two other women there who were interviewing for the same position at the same time.

I went to church for both services to get a "feel" for their styles of worship. It was with a denomination that was nowhere near my home church. But since I had been in the faith arena for a number of years now, I was familiar with the tenants of most major religions. Also at the service, they sang a song I was quite familiar with. Every though it had been arranged quite differently, I knew the hymn.

After service, my host family took me out to eat before I boarded a plane to come back home. They promised to let me know one way or another. That was in February. In May I left to go out of the country to visit some friends. I had not heard anything from the church regarding the position so I figured I didn't get it. I said to myself that when I got back from vacation I would continue my search. Something was bound to turn up. God had already worked it out. I just had to keep looking. In the meantime, I had been on two vacations with the job interviews and I was excited to see where he was taking me next.

So I went on vacation out of the country in May. Every few days, I would stop by an internet café and check my email. You could imagine my surprise when I got an email from the church offering me the position. I told them I was out of the country on some much needed rest and relaxation and I would call them when I got back into the States.

And when I got back, they overnight a contract for me to sign and send back. The contract contained everything we had talked about during the interview except for one thing. The salary was the exact same salary I had made ten years earlier. I mulled this over for some time. I knew what expenses I was still responsible for at my home. This was to be a contractor position for a specific time. After I fulfilled the terms of my contract, I would be headed back home.

Then I was reminded of God's math. Man's math says $1+1=2$. God works out of His abundance and not out of poverty. $0+1=$ all I would need. I am 0 and God being everything else. So I arranged to start my new position the first day of the next month. The new position was a thousand miles away.

I recommended someone to take my place at my home church and I made arrangements to get on the road. I got my old car tuned up and new tires. I told my mechanic I wanted to make sure it got me there, but he told me he wanted to make sure it ran once it got me there. I left my youngest son in the house since he was the last one to leave home. He was taking the "circuitous route" to growing up.

The pastor of my home church did a commissioning ceremony with me during my last Sunday before I got on the road. The day before, my church family did a toast (and not a roast) party for me at the church. I took three days to drive down to Dallas. I had never been in that part of the country. I always thought Texas was West but I found out it is in the South. I guess that is true when you think of Juneteenth starting in Texas.

The weather was perfect. I packed a few clothes, some books and a TV. Anything else I needed I just figured I could buy once I got there. I told the church I would need to stay with a host family until I could afford to move out on my own. I stayed with a nice older couple for a month. Then I rented a room for an older widow woman for a couple of months. Nothing felt like home. I was used to living in a house. Now I was relegated to one room with no privacy. So eventually, I rented an apartment. The first night, I went and bought a blow up bed. Then I began to prowl thrift stores for bare necessities. My thought was to donate everything when I got ready to come back home.

I can't tell you that everything was easy. It was not. But I learned more about myself during those difficult times than I would have learned had everything been very easy. And I made some lifelong friends. The people in that faith community learned to love me like I had never been loved before. And the same can be said of me. I learned to love them with all I had.

And oh yes, the door I saw in my vision, was the exact same door to my office in Dallas. Is God awesome or what?

Then came a time when I was returning back to the church from a hospital visit. I came in the side door that was closest to the parking lot. This door did not have a camera on it but it was closest to my office. I tripped and fell at this door in the parking lot. I tried to get up and couldn't. I realized no one could see me and it was in the middle of the afternoon. That meant that everyone was back from lunch. This church is on a major expressway hidden by shrubbery. Even someone driving down the street couldn't see me sitting on the parking lot between the cars.

I had been in Dallas for over a year. My initial contract was for one year. We were looking at doing another contract and the church was trying to work out funding.

As I sat there I had a talk with God. I had not been to a doctor since I had been in Texas. I probably needed to see a neurologist to assess my current situation with Multiple sclerosis. He told me it was time to come home.

This church was full of resources. When I came down for the interview,

I stay with a retired airline pilot. A member passed and his wife gave me their bed, table, chairs and lamps since she was moving from a house into an assisted living apartment and she didn't have room for all of her furniture. The pieces were so functional I didn't want to leave them. But I knew I couldn't drive a truck back. Again God came to my rescue.

The church decided to fly me home, ship my car home on a car carrier and ship my furniture by a moving and storage company. And this is how things happened. I arrived in a neighboring town but wouldn't get home in time to receive my car and furniture, so my brother-in-law and brother came and got me and brought me home. I got home at one-thirty p.m. My furniture got home at two-thirty and my car got home at four-thirty, all on the same day. WOW! You talk about timing.

Yes, I came back and started at my home church as the parish nurse again and I went to see a neurologist. The neurologist had treated my daughter the year I left for Dallas. I liked her bedside manner and she was a Multiple sclerosis researcher. She would eventually put me on disability.

I could make the most of that situation or I could be sad and make things worse. I chose again to trust God and His infinite wisdom. I was learning to walk by faith and not by sight.

My daughter was spending a large amount of her time taking care of her father. He was getting old and really needed someone to see after him. After a while I could see this was taking its toll on her. She was trying to be his caregiver, take him to his doctor appointments, etc. She also had a full-time job and was trying to go to college.

A couple of times she brought all of his possessions over to my house and we stored them in the basement. He had been evicted and was staying either with her or with another friend.

Finally, there came a time when he seemed to be stable. Everyone was breathing easier. He still refused to take any medication and refused to get any counseling. She had helped him get his own apartment in her apartment complex.

One day she called to tell me he had been walking to the store in inclement weather. He had slipped on some ice. He had fallen and broken his upper arm on his dominant side. She had taken him to the orthopedic surgeon and they would do surgery in a couple of days. I got all the details and told her I would meet her in the surgical suite the day of his surgery.

When I arrived, I could tell he was struggling. He was terribly afraid of going under anesthesia. I tried to assuage his fears but he wouldn't believe me. When he went into surgery, I took our daughter to eat. I told her to call me if anything changed. Otherwise they would keep him for a few days, give him some physical therapy and send him home.

The next call was from our daughter and she was frantic. She said they had "lost" her father. Apparently he had discharged himself out of the hospital against medical advice. No one knew when he left or where he was going when he left. Our daughter went to see him and he was not there. I made some follow-up phone calls to the hospital but to no avail. And to make matters worse, he was within his medical rights to do so.

Just about the time I show up at the hospital, he had returned to the hospital through the emergency department. They readmitted him. He wanted to sign himself out again. This time emergency psychological services intervened. The put him on a seventy-two-hour hold. Then they got an emergency transfer order to an older adult mental health unit.

When I saw him there, he was on tranquilizers and still having a hard time. He was confused, disruptive and violent. The hospital did what they had to do to make sure he didn't hurt himself or anyone else. Again, I had to go to probate court to force him to receive treatment. I hated doing this to him but I just couldn't see any other way to get him the help that he needed.

Our daughter was there everyday between work and school. She was stressed to the max herself. Our son came to see him sporadically. I came often but not everyday.

There came a time when he was stable and the hospital made plans to discharge him. I remember how stressed our daughter was the last time we went through this. She started having seizures and she wound up with a diagnosis of epilepsy. I didn't want her to start having seizures again. She was still on anti-seizure medication, but I knew this stress was not conducive to her or her father's well-being.

In some of my previous conversations with God, I had mentioned that if we were separated and never divorced and if he ever needed me in the future because of sickness, then I would come back, get him and take care of him until one of us died. I believe that God was putting me to the test. I told our daughter that I would take care of her father from that point on. She asked me if I was sure, and I said yes.

All of our children knew of my husband's alternative lifestyle. It seemed to affect our daughter least of all. It affected our son most. He once asked me if I knew of his father's lifestyle. I assured our son that it was nothing he could tell me about his father that I didn't already know.

So from that point on, I would take my husband to his doctor's appointment. His arm healed very well. He became much calmer. I would take him to the grocery store once a week. We started to have a routine where on the days I took him to the grocery store, he would take us out to eat. I would go wherever he wanted to go. Also, whatever else he needed, I would take him to get that as well. Over the next couple of years we developed an amicable relationship.

I knew I was making progress in this journey called "life." My oldest son's father was having outpatient eye surgery. He was now divorced and asked people on Facebook "who could pick him up and take him back for a checkup the next day?" Immediately my son responded with: "Why not ask Mom?" In other words, you know she will do it.

And so after over thirty years, I brought him to my house, put him in the spare room, made him comfortable and told him to call me in the morning. But if he needed anything, to please just call my name or ring my phone and we both went on to sleep.

The next morning, he took me to breakfast before I took him back for his post surgical appointment. His doctor said everything was fine and cleared him to go back to his home by himself.

I took him to his home and we said our goodbyes. I thought to myself, my children must really know me. I am always trying to represent Jesus here on Earth. That was a small thing to do for the father of my oldest son. There is no animosity between us. I see the relationship he has with his son, his church family, etc. We all are growing. This is a process.

Once I took over care of my husband, my daughter could focus on finishing her education. It finally came a time when she was to graduate. I decided to throw her a graduation party at our home in the backyard, right after graduation. She was happy that this journey was finally over.

My sister decided to bring my mother to the graduation. Imagine that! And I decided to bring my husband, her father, to the graduation. He was on some new medicine. He was very "spacey" but cooperative. I picked him up. He had gotten himself dressed. We all met at the university where the ceremony was to be held. I was happy since this was the same school that had named me "Most Distinguished Alumni." I felt like she was carrying on a time-honored tradition.

My mother was unable to stay for the entire graduation ceremony because of her health. So I helped my sister put her in the car and told them to go to my house where we would be having a graduation celebration. I hurried back to the ceremony just in time to see my daughter walk across the stage. I was thrilled!

After the ceremony, we all met outside the arena where we congratulated our daughter. Her father was excited for her also. We all promised to meet up at my house for the party.

When we arrived at my house, we were greeted by a wonderful sight. There sat my husband's brothers, all of them. They actually came from out of town for this most auspicious occasion. I had no idea they were coming and neither did my husband.

I suspect my daughter did but she didn't tell anyone.

I came right in and began to set up everything. I had bought everything the day before. I asked everyone to bring something to share with eight people. Everyone complied.

What a wonderful day we all were having. Generations were there to wish my daughter congratulations on this milestone. Even my first husband was there and he agreed to spin records for everyone. We had different age groups. We had different nationalities, different ethnicities, etc. But all were having a great time. I even got out and danced a bit.

And when it was time to leave, my ex-husband agreed to take my current husband home and make sure he got in okay. He said it would save me a trip. I was glad because I was tired but happy. And life returned to its old routine.

When your heart designs the destination, your mind will

automatically draw a perfect map so follow your heart!

Chapter 6: The Call That Would Change My Life

"God gives his toughest battles to His strongest warriors or He makes His strongest warriors using His toughest battles. Either way, I was on my way to being invincible!"

I have had many firsts in my professional life. As a result, I have received many awards of distinction for my work in nursing. I was the first African American Parish Nurse/Faith Community Nurse in our city. I was awarded the "ImageMaker" award for Medicine/Health. I was the first Nurse Health Physicist in the country. This came about through a friendship I had developed with another nurse when I was teaching nursing. After I concluded teaching, she and I hadn't seen each other in almost ten years.

During our time of professional separation, she went to Germany to learn all about the effects of radiation toxins on our bodies at the cellular level. She and her team developed indoor mitigation strategies with "green" nanotechnologies. She was the "gold medal" winner for her application of these applied strategies. She, along with engineers and doctors, had developed a course to teach people how to mitigate the harmful effects indoors and teach health care how to take care of our patients using this new technology.

As a result her project, H2H2020, was selected to be featured "in residence" at Teacher's College at Columbia University. She had made plans to go to experience the feature and invited me to attend. One morning she picked me up and we drove to East Cleveland for a three-day intensive training on electromagnetic radiation, its effects on the body and other harmful indoor toxins. Then we spent the last day on how to mitigate their harmful effects. In fact, we actually went to another nurse's house and brought down his indoor radiation to an acceptable level using the strategies.

When we returned to Cincinnati I invited her to one of our Black

Nurses Association of Greater Cincinnati monthly meetings. From this offering, she gave our ten scholarships named the Marsha D. Thomas Healthy Homes Scholarship for a mini-course on indoor toxins and mitigation. Several members of our association took advantage of this opportunity.

An opportunity came up to present new learning at the annual conference of the National Black Nurses Association in New Orleans. I contacted my sponsor and she submitted the paperwork. And wouldn't you know it? She was accepted. She flew down to the conference and presented her new home care model. It was very well received. She was able to get a sponsor. I was so happy for her!

Now upon her return from the New Orleans conference, she began to look for other opportunities to share her groundbreaking work. And wouldn't you know it, Teacher's College at Columbia University was having their annual conference. They asked her to be a part of this conference. She immediately agreed. Then she called me and offered me the opportunity to be part of her team who would present at the conference at Columbia University. Naturally I was ecstatic to be given such a wonderful opportunity.

She began briefing me and bringing me up to speed on what we would be doing during our presentation. She had also arranged to be the opening seminar for the entire conference. She introduced each of us on the team to each other. We talked about how people reacted when their homes were toxic.

Because this information is so important to the health of you the reader, I wanted to add this educational synopsis for you right here in this book. It's as if you are being given the gift of an insider's look that can dramatically decrease your susceptibility to the harmful effects of toxic radiation.

In our team meetings, we discussed how high levels of toxicity in the home can produce things such as seizures, headaches, high ant invasion, etc. Then she talked about the damage done by cell phones and she gave a very visual demonstration. Then she showed how a small nano flat battery, taped on your cell phone, could protect you. She also talked about the emerging research being published in scholarly journals regarding the effects of harmful radiation from our world of technology.

She introduced the B-DORT, or Bi-Digital, O-Ring Test. This test was developed by a doctor in Japan. My colleague/team leader could demonstrate the damage done by just holding and using a wireless microphone, and then show the mitigating effects once nano technology was applied.

In the meantime, she had reduced the toxins in my home a couple of years before, when she would sometimes come down and spend the night with me. She showed me the dangerous levels in my home, and then she lowered them to a "safe" level. She said she couldn't be in my home without the mitigation and neither should I.

She was always encouraging me to sleep with my head at the foot of the bed. She said it was too much electricity running through the wall at the head of the bed. Truly we plug everything into the wall at the head of the bed—lamp, alarm clock, radio, etc. Next she told me that you sleep on metal springs, box springs. She said "We are being tased all night long." It affects everybody but is quite dangerous for the very young, the very old and the very sick. She said that as we get sicker, we eventually will receive a hospital bed. We also plug this into the wall at the head of the bed. Our patients are being bombarded with electro radiation all night long. (And we wonder why they have a stroke in the middle of the night and die.) Her work has been documented and verify by the likes of Columbia University. Currently she is "Scholar in Residence" at Columbia University.

It was a three-day conference with the kick off on a Friday night. Eventually the entire team made it to the hotel and then we all went off to the conference. I had asked our team leader about her return plans. She said that we would leave immediately after the conference. We would drop one doctor off in Washington, D.C., then head straight back to the Midwest. I told her that was good because I knew my husband had a doctor's appointment the very next day. My plan was to take him to his appointment.

The week before I left for New York, I got some heartbreaking news. My husband's younger brother, the one right after him, was found dead in his garage, on the floor, with the garage door open on the coldest day of the year in February. No one knows all the details but it was eventually ruled an accidental death and not a homicide.

My husband was devastated. He and this brother were extremely close. And they were extremely competitive. The fact that there we so many unknowns really got to my husband. He was very upset when he called me with the news. I told him I would come and take him to the store to get him a new set of clothes to wear to his brother's funeral.

I picked him up and we immediately went to a men's specialty store. My husband was quite obese and I wanted him to look decent at the funeral. We had to get the suit altered and it wouldn't be ready for a few days. It was a beautiful blue suit. He seemed happy with the way it made him look. He hadn't been home, back to his birthplace, in almost 10 years. He would be seeing family and friends he hadn't seen in a long time. My daughter and I had agreed to drive him up. I also would be seeing people I hadn't seen in quite some time.

We picked up the suit after it was altered and I got my husband his weekly groceries. We went out to eat. I could tell he didn't have a lot of people he could confide in. I was probably one of only two people he could talk to about his feelings. He believed I could understand since I had received a similar phone call about my younger brother a few years back. Yes, I knew how it felt to have the rug pulled right out from under you!

A few days before the funeral, my girlfriend called me with the invitation to go to the conference at Columbia University. My daughter told me to go on to New York with the team and she would drive her father to her uncle's funeral. I knew my husband had a doctor's appointment that following Monday. I told my husband I would be back from New York by then and I would take him to the appointment. I really wanted to speak with the doctor regarding the increasing pain in his legs and feet.

He had been seeing a podiatrist for the past six months, but the pain had not subsided. In fact the pain was intensifying. He was still walking normally but complaining about "pins and needle" feeling in his lower extremities. The podiatrist had diagnosed him with diabetic neuropathy. Now he wanted his primary care doctor to confirm that he indeed did have diabetes. No test had showed this so far. Fortunately, my specialty was cardiac and I know as much about diabetes as I know about heart disease. So I could reassure my husband that whatever his final diagnosis was, we could handle this.

To wrap up the conference, the entire team went to the world famous restaurant Sylvia's for a scrumptious dinner. The food and ambiance was all that I had heard it was. There were two sides to the restaurant. We sat on the side with Christian jazz music. I had never heard music like this before. It was music to my ears.

Then the waiters/waitresses asked: "Who had a birthday that month?" And wouldn't you just know it, it was my birthday month. So I was treated to a jazz rendition of "Happy Birthday" with piano accompaniment. I was thrilled. I felt so special. Even though I had the death of a beloved brother-in-law hanging over me, I was able to let loose and just enjoy myself.

We returned to our hotel and packed our suitcases. Again, I asked our team leader when we would be leaving and when I would arrive back in my home city? Everyone seemed to be on "coast" mode. The conference had been intense and everyone was just relaxing.

She said she wanted to stop in Washington, DC, for a day or two and stop in Pittsburgh for a day or two. I was adamant that I needed to get home the very next day. I explained that my husband had a doctor's appointment and I needed to be there to hear what they had to say.

Since no one was in a hurry to get home, she suggested we find a cheap airline ticket. This sounded fine to me. Immediately we started looking online for a ticket. At first all the tickets from all the airlines were cost prohibitive. Finally after many hours, we found a "red-eye special" that would get me home in the afternoon.

I called the front desk and asked about service to the airport. I was in another state altogether. They gave me the name of a service that would pick me up at four forty-five a.m. All day I kept hearing a little voice say: "You need to get home. He is sicker than you think."

I called my husband to make sure everything was okay. That is when I found out he did not go to the funeral. He said, "I just didn't feel like it." I understood perfectly. I like to remember people the way they were when they were up, laughing and joking and not lying in a coffin. Lately I have gotten in the habit of not even going up to look at the body. That is not how I pay my respect.

When my service arrived to take me to the airport, I was already at the door. I had already said goodbye to my comrades. We promised to keep in touch. I got to the airport, got through security and got on the plane. Then we were airborne. The flight was uneventful. We landed in

Chicago and I had a three-hour layover. I had missed my connecting flight and I had to wait for another plane to take me the last leg of the journey.

Again, I called my husband to tell him that I had been delayed in Chicago. I was going to suggest that he catch a cab to the doctor's office. I had already made arrangements for our youngest child to pick me up at the airport and take me home. There I would drop my luggage, get in my car and head straight to the doctor's office.

As I explained all of this to my husband, he calmly told me he was not going to the doctor that day. He said he just didn't feel like it. I knew that once he had his mind made up about something, no amount of talking could persuade him to change his mind. So I told him to just call me if he needed me and we would make another appointment tomorrow, after I arrived home. He agreed that would probably be for the best. He sounded fine but I still couldn't get that still voice out of my head telling me he was sicker than I knew.

I landed. Our son picked me up and took me home. I mentioned my suspicion about his father's health. He said to keep him informed when I found out anything.

When I got home, I called our daughter to let her know I was back home. She began to tell me about how her father had called her and told her that he was not going to his brother's funeral. He said he just didn't feel like it. This was becoming his "pat" answer for anything he didn't want to do.

So I went to bed early after a long day of travel. I was awakened early the next morning with a call from him. He said he was on the floor and he couldn't walk. I said I would be right over as soon as I got up and got dressed.

I cleaned up as quickly as I could. I fed the dog and let him out to do his business. Then I quickly got in my car and traveled to his apartment.

What awaited me was more than I had anticipated.

He indeed was on the floor, lying on his back with his legs bent. Fortunately, he was able to crawl to the door and unlock it before I got there. He was a miserable sight. His hair was unkempt. His body was not clean. He hadn't shaved in several days. And his apartment was *filthy*.

I asked him what happened? He said his legs were too painful to stand on. I told him I would take him to the hospital. He reiterated that he couldn't stand so I called 911.

When 911 got there, they had to decide how to get him out to the ambulance. Luckily there were several husky men who responded. He was strapped onto a gurney and taken outside. I told them I would follow and meet them at our large teaching hospital. I knew they gave good care there and if anyone could determine what the problem was, I believed they could.

My mind was racing as we traveled quite a distance to get to this Level One trauma hospital, the only one of its kind in this region. In fact, we passed up several hospitals, which were much closer, but I was determined to get him the best care possible.

You see, out of all the people he could have called, he called me. This meant something to me. This meant that we had a level of trust that had been forged over many a rough road and many hardships. But I guess at our core, we truly were different people than when we were living together.

After some preliminary tests, he was seen by a nurse practitioner. She made the decision to send him home with instructions to follow up with his primary care physician. He was fitted with a pair of crutches that didn't help very much. His legs and feet still hurt him something awful. It was so painful to watch him try to maneuver to the car.

I arrived at his house before eight a.m. Neither one of us had any breakfast. It was afternoon when we left the hospital. He told me he was hungry. I asked him where he wanted to eat and he told me. It was a sit down restaurant. Again, it was difficult to watch him try to drag himself in to be seated.

My BFF number 2 had called with a routine check in. When I told her all that had transpired she said she would grab her husband and meet us at the restaurant. Despite his pain, we had a great time, just the four of us, laughing, joking and reminiscing. The service was fast and the food was delicious. I was feeling very optimistic about all our futures.

I told everyone at the table that I had made the decision to bring him back to my house, to take care of him. Even though I lived in a two-story, I felt if we could just get him up to one of the bedrooms where there was a bathroom right next to it. Also, I had my girlfriend get an oversized wheelchair from a second-hand store. It was very sturdy. They brought it to the restaurant and transferred it to my car upon our departure. She also promised to come over to my house and cut his hair since it hadn't been cut or combed in a long time.

Next we went to the pharmacy to get his prescriptions filled. Then we went to a thrift store. I needed to get him some warmer clothes. He was still in shorts and a T-shirt with a coat and sandals. It was much too cold for that. Officially it was still winter, according to the calendar. Lastly, he told me to go to his house. He had made a large withdrawal thinking he was going to his brother's funeral. He figured he and our daughter would rent a car and would stay at a hotel. He didn't want that amount of money lying around his apartment and mostly everyone had seen him leave by ambulance and they had not seen him return. He just didn't want to take that chance.

I did as he asked and I gave the envelop to him. After little hesitation, he asked me if I would keep it for him until he got settled and found out about his legs.

When we got to my house, I was so worn that I locked my purse up in the car. I had already assisted him into the wheelchair and we were sitting in the garage. I went next door to borrow a knife to see if I could "jimmy" the lock, but to no avail. Then I remembered I kept a spare key in the garage hidden. As I rummaged for the key, I said a silent prayer, thanking Him for His provision and guidance as we navigated these new waters.

Luckily, a few years earlier, my house had been modified with some accessibility features. There is a steel ramp that goes from the house down into the garage. I used this to push him up into the house. Next, I moved some furniture around so he could easily navigate between the kitchen, dining room and living room.

Our next hurdle was getting him up thirteen steps. I had a chair lift installed a couple of years earlier. It had been repaired at least two times in one year. Finally when it quit working the third time, I made the decision not to get it repaired again. I had noticed that when I used it, I became much weaker. I couldn't do a lot for myself. Also, it had a weight limit and he was over that limit significantly.

Luckily, his arms were still strong. He got himself out of the wheelchair and onto the steps. Next he grabbed the railings that had been installed for me to use when using the steps. They were very sturdy. He was able to pull himself up the steps and lie on his back and drag himself along until he got to the chosen bedroom.

I was able to bring the wheelchair up to his room. I helped him into it. Then he was able to transfer himself into the bed. He said it felt strange to be sleeping under the same roof with me. It felt strange to me too. I had never foreseen this coming. I made sure he was comfortable. He wanted a radio to keep him company since there was no TV in that bedroom.

I made the decision that it would be easier for me to take care of him in my house. Therefore I would ask our children to move everything over here. I would see about breaking his lease once I took him to see his primary care physician and get a preliminary diagnosis.

Funny how the human mind works when you are in "crisis mode" and this was a crisis. He was unable to walk. I had to see to his needs. I cooked, cleaned, ran errands, emptied urinals, etc., all with a smile on my face. Past hurts went out the window. Here was a human being who needed my help.

I was able to get an appointment with his doctor for four days later. We would just have to muddle through for four days. In the meantime, I woke up early every morning. I would let the dog out, feed and water him and make sure the dog was okay. Then it was off to make breakfast for my husband and myself. Then I would sit with him and talk with him about something positive. I really was trying to alleviate any fears he might have about the future. I was working on short-term plans because I didn't know how things would turn out from day to day.

My girlfriend came over the next day to cut his hair. It hadn't been combed in over a year. He agreed to let her cut it all off. It filled up a trash bag. We all three laughed about it. We all were trying hard to be the people that God wanted us to be to fellow human beings.

And finally the day arrived for him to go to the doctor. One thing I didn't count on was him not being able to walk. He had been steadily getting weaker. I said I would have to use a transport service or an ambulance service. I made several calls to some companies I knew. The cost was exorbitant with each one. I sat on the side of the bed after I got us fed and I got myself dressed.

One by one, I ticked off my options. My brother-in-law was too old and weak. My husband was dead weight.

We had to get him downstairs and into the car. I could use the wheelchair once we got him down the steps but how to get him down the steps was my dilemma. Our son couldn't do it by himself. He would definitely need help. My daughter couldn't lift that kind of weight and besides, the children were at work/school during the day. It was no one on the street to help. Again, I bowed my head and asked for guidance and wisdom.

My husband was in his bedroom putting on his clothes. About that time I heard a loud thud. I scrambled to see what had happened. I found him sitting on the floor. He said he fell out of the bed and he couldn't move. Again, I called 911. Again they took him back to the teaching hospital. Again, I followed the squad. But this time they admitted him.

They wanted to keep him to see what had caused this man to stop walking after all these years. They needed to find out what was causing pain that was so excruciating that he couldn't bear to put any weight on either leg or foot. All of his vital signs were normal so they were definitely puzzled.

I stayed with him all day at the hospital. I talked to his teams of doctors. We reviewed all of his preliminary tests. Nothing gave any indication of what was happening inside of his body. It just seemed like his body had turned on itself. He was apprehensive. I assured him that I would be there every step of the way. The doctors were very accommodating. They always tried to let us know what they knew, which right then wasn't very much. I stayed and helped him order his meals and to make sure he was comfortable and settled in. I told him I had to go home to see about my dog and to get some rest myself. This had certainly been a *trying* week.

After I got the dog settled in and myself cleaned and dressed for bed, I had a long talk with Our Creator. I was feeling so many mixed emotions. I was running on pure adrenalin. I was confused and conflicted. I needed guidance and direction.

I fell into a peaceful and easy sleep.

Anyone who knows anything about Multiple sclerosis knows this diagnosis comes with myriad complications, the least of these being bowel and bladder challenges. That is where I was that night. In the middle of the night, I jumped straight up to run to the bathroom. My bladder was full and it was screaming for relief.

When the firemen had come in the previous morning to get my husband off the floor and take him to the hospital, we had pulled a walker/rollator into my bedroom out of the way. When I came in that evening, I was too tired to move it and just left it where it was, sitting between my bedroom and the bathroom. Without a night light, I didn't see the rollater there when I was running to the bathroom.

I collided with the walker, tripped and fell right shoulder first, into a weight-bearing wall, hitting a stud. Or as I am fond of saying, I had a "fight" with my wall—and my wall won. The dog had excellent reflexes so he was able to get out of the way as I started to fall. His sleeping place is right by my bed but he had been sleeping there for years so I knew to avoid him. The walker was new.

When I could collect my thoughts, I was lying in a heap on the floor with an aching shoulder. I noticed as I tried to right myself and straighten myself out, I didn't have a lot of use of my right arm and it was beginning to throb.

I was able to wriggle into a pair of jogging pants and ease a coat over my arm and shoulder. Two things I knew: (1) the dog was not going to let any strangers into the house and (2) I need to have my arm looked at by a health care professional. So I grabbed my purse, put my cane in the other hand, hobbled down the steps and out the door to get into the car.

It had taken me about three hours from the time of my fall until I could start the car. The sun was just beginning to break over the horizon. It wasn't a lot of people on the street at that time of the morning on a Saturday. I was grateful for that.

If you have never tried to drive with just one hand, even if you have an automatic, it is difficult. My gearshift is on the column so I had to try to ease my left hand over the steering wheel to shift gears and start the ignition. Fortunately, I was finally on my way. And guess what? I again passed up all the hospitals that were closer to get to our large teaching hospital. Even though you are triaged differently when you arrive by squad than if you arrive yourself, I was seen within thirty minutes. Next I was rolled into X-ray. And my worst suspicions were confirmed—I had a broken rotator cuff of the right shoulder.

I had just been at that hospital the previous year for a very bad flare-up of MS. The health care team was suspecting that my falling was a result of another flare-up. Therefore the neurology team decided to admit me to Neurology for observation. I told them my fall was a result of me being tired, stressed and incontinent. I don't think they believed me or else they just wanted to make sure.

Eventually, transport came to take me to my room. Once there, my admitting nurse came to do my assessment. Then and only then could I order some lunch.

I have never taken my husband's admitting information out of my purse. So I reached and got it using my non-dominant hand. Was I in for a surprise? I was told I couldn't move my right arm at all. The break was so clean that the orthopedic team felt they could risk not giving me surgery if I could keep that arm from not moving or else immobilized. Of course I was willing to give this option a try first. I really didn't want to have to have surgery at all if possible.

I called my husband and was he surprised. He also was sad. He felt that he had worn me out so much that I had fallen because of the added burden. I assured him that accidents do happen and no one could have foreseen this.

I was in a semi-private room. I had a nice roommate. She had been there for several days and was looking forward to going home soon.

My husband and I got in the habit of calling each other several times a day. We talked about our family, this change in our lives, what our views were, etc. We also talked about our diets. He had been placed on a diabetic diet and he was not real happy with his food choices. I was on a regular diet that meant I was free to order anything I wanted.

I told my admitting nurse that my husband was in the same hospital but on a different floor because of a tentative diagnosis. You know what this wonderful nurse did? (I always say: "Nurses think with their hearts.") When she got a break she agreed to put me in a wheelchair and take me to visit my husband. This sounded like a wonderful idea to me.

I have a first cousin who went to high school with me. We were in the same homeroom because we have the same last name. We are brother and sister's children. I lost track of her after high school. I had only seen her about three times in almost forty years. But a year before these events, we bumped into each other through her children and had resumed a very close relationship.

When I was admitted to the hospital, I called her so she could come and get the keys to go to my house twice a day and let the dog out and in. Also he had to be fed and watered. The mail had to be checked, curtains closed, etc. I didn't know it then, but when we hung up she called my sister who was borne right behind me and my BFF No. 2.

Later on that evening the nurse came in with a wheelchair and told me we were going for a trip to see my husband. As she was assisting me into the wheelchair for the ride, in walks my sister, my cousin and my best friend. The nurse told me she was taking all of us up to see my husband. She took us through the employee's entrances, the back way.

When we got to my husband's room, they were doing personal care on him. I was allowed to go in since they were almost done. He was in a private room. Everyone else stood at the entrance to his door until the caregivers left. Within five minutes, transport picked him up to go and get an MRI. Everyone laughed and joked with him as he was being wheeled down the hall. As I look back on this scene, it seems surreal now.

Everyone came back down to my room and visited with me. After they left, that wonderful nurse came to see me regarding an idea she had. She was wondering if I would mind if they moved my husband in with me now that my roommate had gone home and I was in a semi private room. I gladly agreed to that idea.

Within a couple of hours, transport arrived with my husband and his belongings. We were officially "roommates." Thus began some of the most wonderful times of my life. And I do believe he felt the same way. The nurses named our room The Thomas Suite. Because of HIPPA, they couldn't put it on the outside of the door but it was all over the inside of our room.

I had asked my cousin to bring my braces for intense physical therapy, some clean and comfortable clothes and my tablet. I was on strict bed rest that meant I had to have assistance whenever I got up, even to sit on the side of the bed. I was a "fall precaution" and they didn't want to take any chances.

Whenever our children would visit, the nurses would take pictures of us. We became something of a sensation at this hospital. This hospital has over four hundred beds and we were the only husband and wife there at the time. I remember hearing people making rounds outside our door and remarking to the staff that "it was a man and a woman in the same room." The staff would assure them they were aware of it and that we were in fact husband and wife.

Thus began a regular routine at the hospital. We especially enjoyed meal times. They became an adventure. Usually our menus would consist of different things. We would confer and decide what we were in the mood for. Then we would order off of both menus and share the foods.

At one time in my nursing career, I worked as a cardiac nurse, which means I am quite familiar with a diagnosis of diabetes. I made sure my husband didn't get any foods that would adversely affect him. He was usually very compliant. I would let him sample something if he wanted, but he couldn't order an entire course. I wasn't going to do anything contrary to both of us getting out of there and being able to resume our normal lives.

From time to time, we would have a conversation with the social worker/discharge planner. We would talk about our next steps. The feeling was we both might have to go somewhere for rehab. We chose a nursing home that had a rehab inside the facility. They started to work on getting us a room together at the nursing home.

During these times, my husband and I would drop all pretense. We would have heart-to-heart conversations. Sometimes we would talk late into the night. On one such occasion, he asked me if I could ever find it in my heart to forgive him? Without any hesitation I replied: "Only under one condition." This got his ire up. He immediately bristled and asked me: "Under what condition?" I immediately replied: "Only if you can forgive me." He became incredulous. He couldn't believe it. I told him it took both of us to tear up our marriage. Yes, we both had said some things and done some things that were unconscionable. Of course he readily agreed that we both needed forgiveness for ourselves and each other. I told him I had forgiven him a long time ago. I told him I had to learn to forgive as I had been forgiven. This meant I had to forgive everyone for everything. I told him it was a tough lesson to learn, but God was leading my life now and I was on an incredible journey.

I can only surmise that he had thought long and hard before coming to the decision to ask my forgiveness. He really didn't know how I would react. I like to think that my recent actions were a good indication of my intentions.

It was finally decided that I did not have a flare-up of MS. My orthopedic team felt that my arm was healing nicely. Of course they based this on X-rays and how often I needed pain medication. I had learned early to keep my shoulder "iced" down and this would mitigate some of the pain. I had three C-sections, impacted wisdom teeth and other surgeries, but nothing—and I do mean absolutely nothing—hurt like bone pain.

Finally the morning came for me to be discharged home. My cousin came to pick me up. Thank God she was not working and was able to do this. I remember that look my husband gave me as I was assisted with dressing, given my discharge summary and placed in a waiting wheelchair for transport out to the car.

But most importantly I remember the look on his face as he told me goodbye and wished me luck. I told him to cheer up. He would be coming home soon. We would see each other again. I promised to visit him everyday no matter where he was. He seemed so sad and I didn't know why. This was not "goodbye." This was just so long. My plan was to come back early the next morning and spend the day with him. I could do this everyday until this crisis was resolved. I could find a way to drive with an immobilized arm, or so I thought.

So my cousin brought me home and got me situated. Physical therapy would come out the next day for their assessment. I would receive physical therapy and occupational therapy on an outpatient basis in my home. My dog was extremely glad to see me and nuzzled me all evening. Then I put us to bed.

Physical therapy showed up the next day and after making their initial assessments, it was determined that I would start receiving therapy the first Monday of the following week, two times per week, one hour each time. I would also received occupational therapy once per week for an hour. This would start with a shower next Tuesday. All was set. Remember the adage: "You want to make God laugh?" Make some plans and see what happens.

The following day after physical therapy assessment, I had an orthopedic appointment for my shoulder. My cousin would come and pick me up, drive me to the appointment, stay with me during the appointment and then drive me back home. Again all was set.

The next day, I got up early. I took care of my dog then I made me a simple breakfast. I was just finishing my breakfast when my cousin let herself in. She sat down and we talked about life and God's provision and His timing. Finally she said she would clean up the kitchen and suggested I go upstairs, clean up and get myself dressed for my doctor's appointment. By this time, I was getting pretty good at negotiating my steps, using the cane in my non-dominant hand. After all, I had been doing it several times over the past couple of days. Also the hospital had ordered me a quad cane and told me not to use my single-point cane. I was not steady enough and it didn't afford me the stability I needed. So I had adjusted to using the quad cane.

At the top of my steps, you pivot to the right and you are inside of my bedroom. Walk ten steps forward and turn left and you are in my dressing room that leads to the master bathroom. I have been living in this house for almost three decades so I know each floorboard intimately. I know the sounds this house makes and I can usually negotiate and navigate it without thinking.

As my cousin made some dishwater to wash a few dishes, I climbed the steps while still talking to her. I pivoted and took five steps. Then I felt myself begin to fall. I couldn't break my fall. My right arm was immobilized. My left hand was holding the cane. I just let myself go and prayed for the best.

My face fell into a large queen's chair made of solid cherry. I fell face first and I wear glasses. Next my body fell but I landed on my left shoulder. My cousin immediately ran upstairs when she heard me fall. She said she had never heard someone fall that hard in her life and she is a nurse also.

My first reaction was to cry like a baby. I knew I had broken more bones on top of my right rotator cuff. I knew I was bleeding all over. My biggest fear was that I would have to go to a rehab facility and that I would never come back to my home or live by myself again. I saw all of my independence pass before my eyes.

My cousin asked me if I could get up? I told her no. She said she couldn't get me up by herself. She said she would have to dial 911 and that is what she did.

As the 911 operator was getting the details, she asked my cousin if I was bleeding anywhere? My cousin said she couldn't see any blood and she asked me if I was bleeding anywhere. I stopped crying long enough to check myself. Funny thing is that I was not bleeding anywhere, at all. Also I didn't hurt anywhere and I told my cousin this.

My cousin was quite upset. I could see it in her face. I could see she was frightened for me. She realized, like I did, the consequences of this newest fall. In other words, this was devastating. She kept assuring me that if wasn't the end of the world, but I felt that it was.

Again the squad ambulance came. This time it was to get me. My neighbors were probably wondering what was going on at our house. The squad had been to my house twice in a month. We probably didn't have this much excitement in a year's time on this street.

My cousin said she would follow the squad. So they closed the door and I told them again to take me to our large teaching hospital. I had just been discharged from there forty hours ago. Wouldn't they be amazed when I showed up there today?

Inside the squad the EMTs did their assessment. They said my vital signs were normal. Imagine that! After everything I had been through, my temp, pulse, respirations and blood pressure were normal.

And when I got to the large teaching hospital, I was triaged differently. I was seen within ten minutes of arrival. This time, I was not seen by a nurse practitioner but by an established emergency room doctor. She started at my head and did a thorough assessment. She checked every tooth to see if any were loose which they were not. Next I went to X-ray where they checked my previously injured rotator cuff. It was still healing nicely with no trauma. They checked my entire body and they couldn't find any evidence of any new trauma.

I was just as confused as they were. You see, I fell so hard, I tore the soles of my shoes off. They were flapping on my feet on the gurney.

And to top things off, what made me saddest was that my husband had been transferred to the nursing home the day before. He was no longer at this hospital.

The decision was made to keep me for observation overnight, and then the next day I was to be transferred to our big rehabilitation hospital. And that is what happened. I called my husband that night and he was very sad for me. I tried to take it all in stride. I was surprised that the worst that had happened is that I had ruined my favorite pair of comfortable shoes. But that was a small price to pay for not breaking any more bones.

The next day, just like clockwork, I was transferred. This was not a picnic. Therapy would start at seven a.m. sharp and it would continue off an on until my last session at four p.m. each day.

I had a steady stream of visitors. Most were so sorry to hear of my present woes. They were glad that my second fall did not result in any new injuries. But they knew how I felt about not being able to get out.

But again my husband and I caught up with each other by phone. We both would have therapy, but most of the time he would refuse his. I begged him to just go along with them. He was quite frustrated that they couldn't pinpoint exactly what was causing his pain.

Sometimes I hated to look at the clock because I knew it was time for therapy. It was relentless and painful. Sometimes it was group therapy but most of the time it was one-on-one with a physical therapist. And when I wasn't having actual therapy, I had exercises that I was supposed to work on. But I was making progress so I was optimistic.

Sometimes my husband and I would talk five or six times a day. We would wake each other up and put each other to sleep with our conversations. Sometimes they were deep, soul searching and sometimes they were light and breezy. Always they involved talk about our menus. We both liked food and the fact that we didn't have to cook really made things special

I have a sister who is an excellent cook and she enjoys doing it. Also one of my favorite kinds of food is Indian. On one particular bright, sunny, grueling day, members of my multiple sclerosis group brought me Indian food for lunch. This even included Mango Lasso. That is the nectar of gods! If you have never had one, you are missing a treat.

After that, I talked to my husband for the sixth time that day. Our fifth conversation had been long and soul searching. He had informed me that his wish was that if his heart should stop, the staff had been instructed to do everything medically possible to restart his heart and get him to breathing again. I told him I was a DNR. (Do Not Resuscitate) This meant that incase my heart stopped or my breathing began to decrease, to only make me comfortable. I did not want any medical intervention to restart my heart and my breathing. He asked me why I wouldn't want to be revived? I told him I was tired of living like this, dragging my legs, using canes, the fatigue, the incontinence, the pain, the cognitive changes and everything else. They were getting to be a bit much. And to top that off, there was no medicine anywhere on the horizon that would restore lost function.

I told him I had a "house not made of hands" that I would live in eternally.

I told him that I was not afraid of death. I was more afraid of someone pushing me down and I couldn't get up without assistance. He remarked how strong he thought my faith was. I told him he could have that same assurance. He just needed to believe and not listen to the world. He told me he was not there yet. Besides I knew that he was grieving hard for his brother and he missed him terribly.

The sixth time he called me, he was giddy. He told me he had just talked to his only sister. Then he told me he had called our daughter and she had answered the phone at work. Usually he would have to leave a message and she would call when she got a break, but not this time. She answered and he laughed with her. Lastly he called me and I remarked that he must be very happy since he had just spoken to the three women in his life. He agreed that this normally never happens. We both only had five minutes to chat before both of our therapies would begin. We agreed to speak later on that evening and we hung up.

My sister brought me a wonderful plate for dinner. I invited her and her friend in to chat with me as I waited for dinnertime to begin. She hadn't been there any longer than five minutes before my phone rang. I put the phone on speaker and laid it on the bed.

My roommate was listening to the news on her side of the room. Her TV was tuned to our local news channel.

The caller on the phone was the emergency room social worker. She called to tell me that my husband's heart and breathing had stopped at the start of his therapy session. She said they had transferred him there by squad after they had worked to regain his heart to beat and him to breathe at the nursing home. She explained that he reached down to try to put on his socks, which the therapist was explaining how to put on and adjust. He told her his chest hurt and he couldn't breathe.

After listening to her for a few minutes, I began to ask where he was at that minute? My sister on the other hand was making jokes. She kept telling the social worker to tell my husband she was going to come out there and get him if he didn't cooperate. The social worker kept ignoring my sister's taunts. She was trying to answer my questions as best she could, but I had a little bit more knowledge than she did about cardiac arrest. I had been a CPR instructor for almost twenty-five years as well as a cardiac nurse.

Finally she agreed to put the emergency room doctor who treated my husband on the phone. After a long wait, which seemed like eternity, I heard this male voice. It is almost surreal now. First, he knew I was a cardiac nurse. He began to give me a blow-by-blow description of what had transpired based on the documentation that came in with my husband.

Then he told me everything they did with/to/for my husband once he arrived in the ER. I kept telling him yes, I knew exactly what he was talking about, especially with tPA, which is the new clot-busting drug. This medicine was developed by the world famous stroke team in Cincinnati, Ohio. And I kept asking where was my husband right then?

I figured, based on everything they were telling me, that they had done all they could for my husband. I figured their next step was to leave him hooked to a machine to help him breath and transfer him to CCU, the Cardiac Care Unit.

Finally, he asked me if I could come to the hospital immediately. I told him I would come as soon as I could. Again I asked him the whereabouts of my husband? I had already made up my mind my husband was not going to live in a vegetative state. I would make the decisions that needed to be made.

By this time my sister had quit joking and my roommate had turned down her TV. We all knew this was serious. The doctor told me he was hesitant to tell me anymore about my husband because he didn't like giving bad news on the phone. I was someone who had dealt with death on many fronts. I was a cardiac nurse, a hospice nurse, a faith community nurse and a nursing instructor. I came from a large family of which a father and two brothers had died. I told him he could tell me anything. I probably could take it. I never even considered the possibility of what he told me next.

His next sentence shattered my world. It ripped a hole in my neat fabric of existence, maybe because, of all of the scenarios I had imagined, this was not one. He said; "Your husband did not make it. He coded at 3:05 p.m. We called the code at 3:55 p.m." They called me at 4:05 p.m.

I screamed and began to cry. My sister fussed at me to shut up. She said she couldn't take me crying. Her friend tried to tell her that I was reacting to the news that my husband of almost thirty years had just died. My roommate, sensing the need for interventions immediately, called the nursing station and they all came running.

Now to say that I had a mixture of emotions when hearing this news would be an understatement. I can still recall some of those emotions many years later. I felt profound sadness, hurt, anger. I was stupefied, incredulous, frightened, just to name a few. How is it that someone you just talked with, joked with, laughed with, is now dead, gone, deceased and expired? And if death could sneak upon him, perhaps it could happen to anyone of us? Now that is a sobering thought.

I was no longer thinking as a nurse, I was thinking as a widow. I realized that my status had just changed. I called my cousin to come and get me and take me to the hospital. She was just as shocked as I was. Next, I tried to call my daughter over the next several minutes. I knew she was on her way to the nursing home to take my husband some sweats so they could work on teaching him to dress in street clothes. Try as I might I couldn't reach her.

I called his sister in his birth city and we cried together. She said she would inform his other living brothers, aunts, cousins, etc. I promised her that when things had settled down, I would give her a call since I had to continue making calls to others.

The nurses sat with me, talked with me, let me express my emotions. Again, they thought with their hearts and not with their heads. It was time for a medication pass, but they stayed with me until I my cousin arrived. Next, we headed to our acute care hospital. The emergency room doctor had asked me to come and sign some papers. I told him I would come right away.

I still kept trying to reach my daughter to tell her what had happened, but to no avail. Maybe this was for the best. I didn't know anything at that moment. I was working on pure adrenalin and not much else. All I could think about was we were laughing at 2:55 p.m. when we hung up the phone. We promised to speak again after dinner. They say he told the physical therapist at 3:05 p.m. that his chest hurt and he couldn't breath. They say his eyes rolled back up in his head and they never got him back even though they coded him three times—once at the nursing home, once in the squad and extensively at ER when he arrived.

I know hindsight is 20/20. I remember thinking to myself, if I hadn't been in the rehabilitation hospital myself, I would have been sitting with him all day. I would have been there when he coded. Or maybe he wouldn't have coded if I would have been there? But I quickly dismissed that idea. God is always right! I just had to cling to that during those difficult moments.

When I got to the hospital, the social worker told me where he was, still in the trauma bay where they had worked on him. Unfortunately our daughter was in there with him. She was crying something awful. I touched his foot and spoke to him. He was still connected to the breathing machine, but all of the machines had been turned off. His eyes were half open but staring and not focused. I kept thinking I should get up and close his eyes, but I didn't.

Soon we were joined by the ER doctor who had pronounced him dead earlier. He was surprised that I was a patient at the hospital and not working there. The next person to arrive was a member of the organ procurement team. I asked my daughter if she wanted to donate? She agreed it would be a good idea. Lastly, I had to make the decision which funeral home I wanted to come and get him.

The previous year, I went to the funeral of the mother of one of my dear friends. The funeral home that did the services had been very accommodating and the price had been reasonable. That is whom they called. The owner called me back that night to say she was in another city because her husband had just had a heart transplant that day. But she agreed to come and see me the next day to make the final arrangements. Then I went back to the hospital. I told them that I wanted to finish my rehab, so they held a dinner for me and had my evening meds waiting.

I probably didn't sleep a wink that night. My mind was a jumble of thoughts. We had a conversation about a year ago about this possibility. He had no life insurance but he had managed to save enough for his burial. He had also put our daughter's name on his account at my urging. This made everything a lot easier.

As I look back over the events of that time in my life, I see God's Hand holding us all. He had me come back early and I moved him back into our home. I took him to the doctor and the hospital, so I was up to date on all of his medical conditions. We were admitted to the same hospital a day apart and were eventually placed in the same room. We spent many hours talking.

Healing took place. I guess neither one of us could die with unresolved emotions. We could be brutally honest with each other. There was no pretense.

How is it that a person falls into a solid wood chair, face first with glasses on, with the dominant arm in a sling and doesn't break anything? There is not one tooth loose. There are no open wounds. Remember, I fell so hard, I tore the soles off my shoes! I keep them as a reminder of what God did for me.

Now I realized that God was just moving me out of the way in His own way. He knows the plans He has for us, plans to bless us and not to harm us.

From then on, I believe I started calling God "Re." "Re" means again. He is the God of Restoration, Redemption, and Rededication. He can Reestablish, Regenerate, Reinvigorate, Reenergize, and Rekindle, Renew, Replenish, Resuscitate and Revitalize, just to name a few. He is the God of

Resurrection. He can make things that are old and dead live again!

My husband's funeral was a festive occasion. Even the weather was perfect. He was a jolly person and I wanted his final tribute to reflect that. My BFF number 2's husband was the officiating person. My first husband did the Scripture reading. In fact, I sat with him during the services. My daughter's friend did my husband's favorite song, "Just Stand." And my eldest, who couldn't make it, wanted "One Sweet Day," which conveyed all of our thoughts, to be sung.

As I was getting ready to leave the repast, someone asked me where I was headed? I told them to my home. They inquired if I was going there by myself. I assured them that I was. I told them my husband was finally at peace and I didn't believe he would ever do anything to harm me. In fact, I was and still am convinced that he is no longer tormented by the demons he had on this Earth. I do believe that I will see him one day, and when that day comes, none of what happened here on Earth will matter anymore.

The storm that was sent to break you is the storm God will use to make you.

Strength doesn't come from the things you can do. It comes from the things you once thought you couldn't do.

Death is not the greatest loss in life. The greatest loss is what dies inside of us while we still live.

CHAPTER 7

I Am Drinking From My Saucer

From Psalm 23: *"...He anointed my head with oil, my cup runneth over..."*

When people ask me how I am doing, I typically say: "I am drinking from my saucer." And they say what? And I have to explain it to them. Psalm 23 says: "I anoint you head with oil, you cup runneth over." I tell them my cup is so full, that it spills into my saucer. Then they get it.

I couldn't see where the events of my life would lead me. But as I have heard old folks say: "I wouldn't take nothing for the journey." I am stronger, wiser, more patient and more understanding.

Six months after my husband died, we got a new grandchild, a baby boy. Our daughter named him after his grandfather, her father. He is just like his grandfather, who he never met or at least that we know of. He is truly a joy, just like my other three grandchildren. Each one is special in their own unique way.

My daughter became quite ill a year after her father died. She battled trying to stay healthy, trying to be a good mother and trying to work until it took a bad turn. I told her she and my grandson had to move in with me, and that is where they are today. She is slowly getting her strength back. She has worked a couple of part-time positions, but her health is still precarious.

My youngest son has had some hard landings. We always say he is taking the circuitous route home. I have seen tremendous growth in him since his father died. His father was in the habit of giving him money whenever he ran short during the month. That well has dried up, so he is learning to depend on himself. My eldest son will be out of the armed services in a few years, and he is making plans for his future post enlistment. I am amazed at God's Hand in their lives. My children have become some of my greatest teachers.

Now about me personally, no I haven't remarried. I haven't met anyone who is that special to me. I don't know what God has in store for me in that area.

Last year I traveled twenty-six thousand miles, both national and international, and I believe I only drove one hundred miles of those twenty-six thousand. I traveled all up and down the East Coast. I went with family to my mother's family reunion in her hometown in the South. I would love to retire to one of those quaint southern towns one day.

I am Project Manager for a clinic my faith community is building in East Africa. I try to go over every year to assess progress. Last year was no exception. While there, we adopted an orphanage and visited there. We took over a donation of brand new braces for children with club feet and delivered them to a clinic in "the Bush." We visited a school of nursing to begin to make linkages so that when the hospital is up and running we will have people to work there.

But one of the main highlights was a birthday I had while over there. We worked very hard the days before and the days after my birthday. But for my birthday, we did absolutely nothing. We took a condo that was fifty feet from the Atlantic Ocean. We sat on the veranda, watched the local fauna and watched the ocean. It was so soothing, healing and spiritual. People fed us without us having to lift a finger except to order what we wanted.

About four p.m., our host came to see how we had fared all day while he went to work in town. He asked if we wanted to put on some clothes and go out for a special night of dining and dancing. I told him absolutely not! I was content to watch the ocean. So he went and brought a big spread of African food along with two bottles of good French wine. And the three of us sat there and ate, laughed and enjoyed ourselves.

Later on that evening, a gentleman came down the beach by himself, playing a traditional African drum. We invited him over to share our meal. He agreed. The night was beautiful. All the stars were twinkling, and they seemed so close you could reach out and touch them. The ocean was roaring in the background. They decided to sing "Happy Birthday" to me. So we clinked our glasses and to the accompaniment of the drum, they sang the "Happy Birthday" song in English.

As I sat listening to the singing, I wondered how life could get any better than that? I was in a foreign country. I didn't have to cook yet I had been treated to some of the best food in the world. I ate fish that up until thirty minutes before was swimming in the ocean. I had wonderful memories of the work that we had been doing and would go on to do for the next few days. We knew we were making a difference in someone's life. I was surrounded by old and new acquaintances that genuinely wished me well.

Even though multiple sclerosis has progressed to the point I need a cane all the time and I have two braces, I was still able to travel such long distances. I have a new neurologist who is a friend of the family. She takes excellent care of me. I am grateful for having found her. Even though I am having slow progression, it is not nearly as bad as it could be.

I currently lead a local chapter of a national organization. I am the president, but I have a wonderful team who are "the wind beneath my wings." The world may see me out front but it is the people behind the scenes that make the difference. Every year we raise scholarship funds for deserving students at our gala. This event is growing and more and more people are coming along side us to assist in some way with this effort.

I speak around the country extensively. My specialty is "Engaging Faith Communities to Change Health Outcomes." I just wrote a faith-based program for the National Multiple Sclerosis Society. Now it will go out for a pilot. I am hopeful that it will be adopted by all of their chapters for implementation.

In the past, I have run faith-based initiatives for American Heart Association, American Diabetes Association, American Cancer Society, our AIDS service organization, and our world famous Children's Hospital, just to name a few.

Next year we are planning on taking nurses, nursing students and other interested parties to our clinic in West Africa. This country was one that was decimated by the slave trade, so while we are there we will visit "The Port of No Return" and other historical landmarks. We will also give and assist in primary, secondary and tertiary care in this country. This trip is the first of many. They are planned each year for as long as I can go. They are open to anyone interested in going to see Africa. I am hoping people will avail themselves of an opportunity to visit "The Motherland."

We all have many defining moments. Usually we think of when we were born, when we became teenagers, when we graduated from high school, college, when we got married, when our children were born, etc. But there are other extraordinary moments that define us also.

I am reminded of an incident that happened in the hospital where my husband and I both were in the same room. I had called the nurse's station and had requested a pain pill for the pain in my right shoulder. It was throbbing and I was miserable. It had been thirty minutes and the nurse still had not brought the medication.

I must have been groaning/grimacing because my husband asked if the nurse had brought my pill yet? I responded with a negative and expressed my desire that I wished she would come quickly.

My husband then rang his call light. When someone answered, he stated that he wanted someone to bring *his wife* her pain medication. He stated that I had called over thirty minutes ago and was in excruciating pain. Wouldn't you know that the nurse was in my room with my medication within five minutes. I immediately swallowed the medicine plus asked for an ice pack. And I finally began to get some relief from the searing pain in my right shoulder.

Later that night, I really meditated on that incident. It had been eons since he had referred to me as *his wife*. And even longer since he had been concerned about me, my health or how I was feeling.

As I contemplated on the significance of the entire hospital experience, I am convinced of two things. One is that incident with the pain medication let me know, without a shadow of a doubt, that God had restored everything the "canker worm" tried to destroy. God was able to bring reconciliation and restoration. It had been almost twenty years since we had that level of closeness and caring between us. And the second thing is that my husband felt he was loved, needed and cared for, as much as I did or more.

Of course God knew we would be separated by death within two weeks of that incident. But in the end, our family unit was "Happy," "Healthy," "Whole," and "Healed."

Only God in His Love and His Infinite Wisdom could do this for us!

I hope you have enjoyed "Moved By Love." Writing this has been cathartic for me. Sometimes I laughed and other times I cried while writing. But through it all, I saw God's Hand weaving a story of an incredible love using flawed human beings to show the world what He is capable of doing if we just move out of the way and let Him.

I choose to make the rest of my life, the best of my life!

And those who were seen dancing were thought insane by those who didn't hear the music.

One day you are going to be hugged so tight until all of your broken pieces will stick back together again.

I am blessed with everything I need. I am working hard toward everything I want. But most of all, I appreciate and thank God for everything I have!

CHAPTER 8

Getting the Assignment

"Getting the Assignment." First off, you don't get the assignment. The assignment finds you. You can't go looking for your assignment. It is already inside of you. You came not only with your assignment but with everything you would need to fulfill that assignment. It was programmed in you before you entered this world. And everything and everyone you will need to fulfill this assignment has already been provided. In fact, they are waiting with baited breath on you to tap those resources.

We are all on assignment from the ancestors. This has been revealed to me again and again throughout my life. I am convinced that I am on loan here, to be a bridge to unite our past and our future.

I am an ordinary woman who is living an extraordinary life. But which of us is ordinary? We were conceived in the mind of God and that alone makes us extraordinary!

I get to speak often in front of large and small crowds. I am unapologetically Christian and pro Black. You see my ancestors wrote a check that I am still cashing today.

I was fortunate enough to send my oldest child to a historically black college. They taught him academics but they also taught him his history. I have always been a proponent of the adage: "If you don't know where you have been, then you don't know where you are going." So it became incumbent upon me to learn my history.

I am the historian of our family. Whenever anyone wants to know our history, they ask me. I am fond of say: "I know where everyone in our family is, living and dead."

A few things that have happened to me over the years bear this out. My grandmother was born with a "veil" over her face, as the old folks say. In current medical vernacular, it means she was born with the placenta over her face. The old folks said this gave her the ability to "see" things that everyone else couldn't see with the natural eye. My grandmother passed this gift on to my mother, who passed it on to me. I passed it on to both of my boys, but my daughter didn't get it.

When I was young, this gift was disturbing to me. But as I got older, it has become a comfort to me, just like a comfortable pair of house shoes that you slip into at the end of a day. You know the ones I am talking about. The ones everyone said you should throw away. But ahhh…they feel so good on your feet after a hard day at work in heels.

One night, I was awakened from a deep slumber to a picture that was unfolding on a wall in my bedroom. I was the only one in the house and the house was dark. A picture was developing on my wall and I was intrigued.

At first, the picture was not clear. Then as clarity began to take effect, I really began to look intently. You see, I became aware of a "sea" of people standing together and they were all looking at me and smiling. They seemed to be standing in rows and the rows were fanning out as the picture got deeper. Everyone in the picture was either brown or dark skin. They were both male and female. Some people had on clothes from different eras and some had their heads wrapped.

It was impressed upon me that all of these were my ancestors. By this time, my father and two brothers had died. But I didn't see them in the crowd anywhere. In fact, I didn't recognize anyone in this massive group. I could only ascertain that these were not recent dead but people who had died a long time ago.

In the front row stood a little girl, about three years old, holding the hand of an older woman. They both were smiling at me and the little girl was waving at me. It was impressed upon me that I would one day join this crowd of ancestors and I would get to come and visit with our descendants.

After a while, the image faded and the wall became white again. The very next day, I went to my mother's to tell her of this strange occurrence. She told me something astonishing. My mother said that our grandmother, her mother, had a baby sister who died when the child was about three years old. My grandmother had never seen her older sister since she was already dead when my grandmother came along. And no one talked about this child.

Since no one talked about her, no one knew what she looked like. I could state emphatically that I knew exactly what this child looked like! Amazing isn't it?

I truly believe that we are all connected somehow and some way to each other—to our past, to our future, to the Earth and to the animals. There is an interdependence that if we could/would recognize it, our lives would be so much richer.

And since all human life originated in Africa, this continent is truly represents all of our connectedness. You can't visit any part of Africa and not feel connected on some level with something over there, be it the people, the animals, the land, the water, our ancestors, etc.

There are thirteen West African counties that were home to the bulk of the slaves who came to America. And most of these countries have a Port of No Return. These are memorials to their countrymen who got on the boats never to return to their homeland again.

Several years ago, while in one of these West African countries and on one of our excursions, our host took us to his country's Port of No Return. We went in the late afternoon/early evening. I had taken a couple of fellow female nurses and a female pastor with me to this country. Our host parked the car and told us to get out and walk down this avenue. He said it would be more meaningful if we walked where our ancestors trod. He would sit in the car and for us to take as long as we wanted to just experience that place.

Earlier that week we had the opportunity to present at a school of nursing in another West African country. After that, in this same country, we had a naming ceremony. My Ebo (African) name is Omebele, which means "The Merciful One." All week long, we called each other by our tribal names and not our American birth names. I have forgotten the other women's names but I still remember mine.

All Ports of No Returns end at the Atlantic Ocean and this one was no exception. The road was about one mile long, a dirt road. And on both sides of the road are large panels depicting some aspect of the slave's journey. We marveled at the craftsmanship and the intricacies of these panels. They seemed to really capture the essence of the horror of that experience.

About halfway down this mile walk was an old slave pen. We chose not to look inside but marveled at it from the outside. It was small, rough-hewn and badly in need of painting. It had iron bars over the windows and doors that had rusted over time, which really lent itself to the eeriness of this place.

The sun was just starting to go down and we were the only people in this whole expanse of time and space. Or maybe it just seemed that way at that time. We all were experiencing this place in our own way.

One member of our party had thought to bring along some plastic baggies. And we all stopped to scoop up some sand and place in the baggies. You see, the sand there is the same color as the red dirt in Mississippi, Georgia and Alabama, not white like the sand on our beaches. That is very significant to me since I was born in Alabama. And it lends credence to the theory that before the great flood, all the land masses were connected.

After I had collected enough sand, I ventured to the water's edge and waded out ankle deep. I wasn't going any further. This was the Atlantic Ocean and the tide had started to come in. So I stood there and pondered the question of why slavery had to happen in the first place?

Then I heard someone call my name, my American name. I looked over my shoulder and answered, "What?" But no one was looking at me. The women were now collecting sand and seashells. I thought to myself that I must have imagined that someone called my name because clearly, no one did.

Then I heard my name again. But this time, it didn't come from behind me, it came from in front of me. It was clearly a man's voice and it was riding the tides of the ocean. Next I became aware of people talking. At first it was two people, then ten, then hundreds, then thousands, all talking at the same time. They were talking in hushed tones. They also were talking in a language that is no longer spoken.

The language they were using was as old as time. But I understood every word they were saying. I can't tell you one thing they were saying now but at that moment I understood them completely.

And above all of the chattering, I heard one lone man's voice clearly. When I looked out over the water, it was not a soul out there; but nevertheless, I heard a voice. And he spoke to my head and to my heart. He said: "Never forget. Never forget what happened here!"

At that moment, I went down to my knees from the weight and the enormity of that moment and I began to cry. Presently everyone came running to see why I had fallen to my knees in the ocean. Even our host got out of the car and eventually arrived.

Everyone asked the same question: "What happened to you?" And all I could say was: "Did you hear him?" "Hear who?" they asked incredulously, like I was a child making up an imaginary friend. I told them: "Didn't you hear that man talking to me?" They all said no they didn't hear him because we were the only ones out there.

Finally our host listened to me tell of all the things that had just transpired and he said: "Those were your ancestors. They were talking to you through the water." Then he added, "That happens all the time" and dismissed it. Well, I couldn't be so cavalier about it? People don't normally talk to me through water, especially people I don't know and I can't see.

So in a few days, I left that country and flew back home. I tucked that experience away in my memory but it never faded. It was truly a significant moment in my life.

The next time I had an opportunity to visit this country was on a business trip. We met with the same host. His country had added new exhibits to The Port of No Return and he was anxious to show them to us.

So one day, when we had some time, we got in the car with him and his driver and headed to the same spot. I reminded him of what had happened to me before and he told me he remembered my experience. And we laughed and hoped nothing like that would happen again.

We stopped at the exact same place we did last time and the driver parked they car. Our host suggested that we get out and visit some of the new exhibits. Immediately sadness and terror washed over me like a torrential rain. The feelings were so powerful that I began to cry in agony. I was just not weeping but howling in unimaginable pain. It was coming in waves, the feelings of sadness, and I was pinned in my seat. I couldn't move. I was immobilized by fear. I was having a visceral experience.

Of course, during this time, everyone in the car was looking at me like I was from another planet. I just keep begging them to "Please don't make me go in there!" That this was a place of such extreme sadness that I just couldn't go in there and to "please, please don't make me." I am not sure I could have gotten out of the car or walked to the exhibit. It was so traumatic just to be in the vicinity and to feel the "waves of sadness" as they washed over me again and again.

I also was aware of my ancestors asking me to "help them," over and over and over again. I was shouting now, "How can I help you!? What happened here was so long ago, I can't do anything about it now!" But they just kept repeating: "Help me, help me, help me!" By this time, I felt like I was losing my mind. Between the emotions and the conversations, I felt like I couldn't breathe, like I was drowning.

Finally our host told the driver to pull away from this spot. We drove about a half mile down this avenue. Finally we came to stop twenty feet from the Atlantic Ocean. Our host got out of the car and came to stand where I was sitting, at the front passenger door. He looked at me as I was trying to get myself together.

And he stated emphatically, "You are right to cry in this place." He said the ground where we were was a mass graveyard.

He told us that all the Africans who were too old, too sick, too weak or deformed in someway, that the slave ship captains thought would not get a good price, were killed at this spot. "That is what you are feeling, all these years later," he said. Wow, how could I have known this unless it had been revealed to me?

To the naked eye, this spot is idyllic. It is picturesque with its red sandy beaches. The ocean is lapping in the background. A large edifice sits on this spot, a tribute to the horror that took place here over and over again. Those souls still cry out for "justice!"

If you can see the invisible, then you can do the impossible!

Don't build a house where you were meant to pitch a tent.

What senses do we lack that we don't know there is a whole other dimension right around us.

CHAPTER 9

Your Future Is So Bright You Need Sunglasses

I send out affirmations every week. I believe in the power of seeing and speaking affirmations. Once you can see it and believe it, then you can achieve it.

One of my favorite is: "Your Future Is So Bright, You Need Sunglasses!" I told everyone to go out a buy a nice, new pair of sunglasses. I also went out and bought myself a pair. I could feel a shift that things were about to take off. I got antsy. I went out and bought myself a new piece of luggage also. Around that time, someone asked me about my hobby. I mentioned to them that I was an avid traveler.

Then an opportunity presented itself to me to do some unlimited travel on a specific airline for 6 months. Now this was not the first time this had happened to me, I spoke it and it manifests itself immediately but it happened so rapidly that I literally had to catch my breathe.

I mentioned the timing to a friend and she suggested that I would be seeing this happen a lot more frequently in my life. And she was right!

A few months back, I was honored as an "Overcomer" for some of the experiences listed in this book. When I was interviewed about this honor, I mentioned that I truly believe that all of us are overcomers. We could not have lived this long and not encountered some "bumps in the road."

I also believe that each and every one of us is not ordinary, but we are extraordinary in our own right. We don't compare the Sun and the Moon. They both shine when they are supposed to.

Each of us was created from the mind of an Infinite and Loving God. That alone makes us extraordinary. We shouldn't let anything dim our shine. Everyone should feel the need to wear sunglasses around us because we shine so brightly.

And we just don't shine when things are going good. We shine all the time regardless. Because we know that it is our mission to bring illumination to wherever we are. We should always let out light shine no matter the circumstances.

I have found that no one comes into my life by accident and everyone who comes into my life brings me a gift. And you can't give without receiving something also.

When I could step back and really analyze difficult times in my life, those were when the greatest growth took place, or my light eventually shown the brightest because it was during those times I had to fight just to find my own light. And it was during those times that the light was so desperately needed, not just for myself but for others as well.

So I want to invite you to go out and purchase a new pair of sunglasses. Why, because some new and exciting things are about to happen in your life. I want you to be open to the possibilities. I don't want you to block your blessings by saying nothing good ever happens to you. You have life and death in your tongue and you will get what you ask for or speak into existence.

Next I want you to get a good set of luggage. You are about to have adventures that you could never have dreamed about. Ask for what you want and be prepared to receive them. Are you wishing for an international trip, well then get a passport! Plan a girl's getaway with a few girlfriends. You might start out just going to the next city for a weekend. Then the next trip will be to another state. You never know, my wish is that one of those trips will be to another country if that is what you want.

What wakes you up at 3:00 am? What are you thinking about when it seems like the entire world is asleep? Maybe it is some business idea or going back to school, etc. But what happens in the light of day, your intellect tells you that dream that is in your heart, that wakes you up, can't be accomplish because you are not smart enough, you don't have enough money, you don't have enough money are a myriad of other excuses pop into you mind.

Hogwash and hogwash some more! It is never too late! I shall say it again. It is never too late. Nothing is the end of the world but the end of the world and it has not come yet.

So join me in this wonderful "symphony" called life. My wish is that you have dreams beyond anything you could have ever imagined.

CHAPTER 10

African American Proverbs & Home Remedies

During my last trip to West Africa, I had resolved to see a traditional healer regarding a physical ailment that had plagued me for years. Everywhere I went, I kept asking to be taken to the home of one of these healers.

My last trip was a business trip and it just seemed like we never got around to me seeing one of these healers. So I came home disappointed in my feeble attempts to rid myself of this pesky problem.

But somewhere in the deepest, darkest night, God spoke to me. He told me that the answer I sought crossed the same ocean our ancestors did and it traveled here to the USA with the slaves. He reminded me that He gave the slaves, our ancestors, a "treasure trove" of knowledge that had not been seen before or since.

He made me realize that the slave owner took the horse to the vet, or the cow to the vet. But the slaves had to take care of themselves. They came to a land they had never seen before. They had to eat food they had never eaten before. The weather conditions were "harsh" to say the least. Sometimes they didn't have shoes, much less adequate clothing. And when they got sick, they had to "heal" themselves.

Our ancestors were already familiar with plants and herbs and their healing power. So they began to experiment until they found something that worked. That knowledge has been passed down from generation to generation. All I need do is nothing but look.
And look I did. I began to ask our elders, especially at churches, for their memories or "recollections" of things their mothers used.

What follows is a partial list of what they told me. (Personal Disclaimer: I have not tried every single one of these remedies. I am simply sharing information and not necessarily endorsing these treatments. I am certainly not an expert in these areas.)

Sometimes a detour will take you exactly where you want to go!

HOME REMEDIES:

- For coughing: lemon, honey, thyme teas
- To sweat out colds: rub Vicks vapor rub on feet and cover with socks, rub on chest and get under the covers to sweat out the cold
- To ward off colds, use elderberry
- For sleep: lavender on pillow, chamomile tea, acupressure band on wrist
- For indigestion: gum, bananas, baking soda, papaya, yellow mustard 1 tsp., ginger, apple cider vinegar
- For constipation: wheat bran applesauce plus prune juice, sugar free chewing gum
- For diarrhea: Archway Macaroon cookies or two coconut cookies, dried coconut, pomegranate, fennel seed tea
- For leg cramps: tonic water, yellow mustard with turmeric, soap under the

bottom sheet near your legs (not Dial or Dove), Pedialyte, pickle juice, V8 juice
- For restless legs syndrome: soap chips in your socks
- For burns: cold water, aloe vera plant, soy sauce, Elmer's glue
- For allergies: Gluten free diet, red bush tea, nettles (steamed)
- For cuts in kitchen: ground black pepper in the wound
- For nose bleeds: keys down the back of neck
- For diabetes: coffee (drink one cup a day to combat Type II diabetes), dark chocolate (one square per day lowers insulin resistance), Stevia extract, oolong tea, cinnamon, cactus, fenugreek herb
- For acne: Listerine, Milk of Magnesia
- Listerine is also used for lice, doggy hot spots, jock itch, planter's wart, rinse hair with Listerine before you wash your hair

- Milk of Magnesia is also used for body odor; wash and rinse off; use as a deodorant
- For nail fungus: corn meal mush – put in bottom of foot bath, add water and soak feet, vinegar and Listerine soak, tea tree oil
- For dandruff: Milk of Magnesia, mayonnaise
- For hot flashes: Black cohosh plus St. John's Wort
- For painful periods: chaste tree berry – Dandelion root (fresh and extract)
- For cholesterol: phylum, fish oils, olive oil, green tea, cinnamon, dark chocolate (but only a little), garlic, ginger, pomegranate juice
- For erectile dysfunction: horny goat weed,
- For hypertension: mood ring (great measure of stress), beets and spinach, magnesium, V8 juice (the low sodium variety), grape juice extract, pomegranate juice, good dark chocolate (5 oz.)

- For eczema: oolong tea, Noxzema,
- Use liquid bandages for skin tags
- For arthritis: aspirin, Brazil nuts, orange juice, Vitamin D, extra virgin olive oil, gin-soaked raisins, Certo (used for home canning to thicken jams), pineapple juice, ginger, turmeric, fish oil, cherries (also used for gout), put soap in hands, put soap chips in pockets – (not Dial or Dove)

If any of you lack wisdom, let him ask of God, that giveth to all men liberally, and upbraideth not; and it shall be given him. James 1:5

(If you would like to contribute to this growing body of knowledge (wisdom), please email me your home remedies and your African American proverbs. We know this generation that is transitioning now is the last generation to remember this knowledge. We want to preserve our heritage. Also, we can save our future by revisiting our past.)

Just like our ancestors came with a store of knowledge to help the nations heal, they also came with wisdom. They translated this wisdom into our proverbs. We may laugh at some of their sayings, but if you look closely or dig deeper, you will find that they hold some critical truths.

<u>African American Proverbs</u>

1. Keep your friends close but your enemies closer.
2. Crème always rises to the top.
3. If you lie down with dogs you wake up with fleas.
4. If you stir poop, some is bound to get on your hand also.
5. When you have one finger pointing at someone, you have three more pointing back at you.
6. Birds of a feather flock together.
7. The apple doesn't fall far from the tree.
8. The darkest hour is just before day.

9. Why buy the cow when you are getting the milk for free.
10. It's your little red wagon; you can push it or pull it.
11. If the shoe fits, wear it.
12. Don't worry about the mule going blind, just sit tight and hold the line.
13. If you play with the dog, he will lick you in the mouth, and if you play with a child, he will cuss you out.
14. When children are young, they are on your lap; when they grow up, they are on your heart.
15. Guests are like fish—all right to have around the first few days, but after that they start to stink.
16. Ain't no fool like an old fool.
17. An empty wagon makes a lot of noise.
18. The noisiest wheel gets the oil.
19. Just you keep living.
20. Been there, done that.
21. The stick you are walking with, I threw down a long time ago.

22. It's a bad wind that never changes.
23. You have two loaves of bread, one under each arm, and still crying for more.
24. We are our brother's keeper.
25. Let go and let God.
26. A hard head makes a soft behind.
27. The more you cry, the less you urinate.
28. What you eat don't make me defecate.
29. God gave you two ears and one mouth so you can listen more than you talk.
30. There is a time and a place for everything.
31. Cleanliness is next to godliness.
32. Everyone has a plan but you are the only one who can make something out of it.
33. Opinions are like assholes—everyone has one and they all stink.
34. The original is always better than the copy.
35. Bad associations spoil useful habits.

36. I brought you into this world and I will take you out.
37. If you are with the crowd, then you are just as guilty as the one who did the wrong.
38. You did the crime, now you must do the time.
39. A family who prays together, stays together.
40. In order to get respect, you have to give respect.
41. Nothing is given; it must be earned.
42. If you don't stand for something, you will fall for anything.
43. Don't cry over spilled milk.
44. That is water under the bridge.
45. Pennies make dollars.
46. Mind your manners and they will mind you.
47. A fool and his money are soon separated.
48. If you can't stand the heat, get out of the kitchen.
49. All that glitters ain't gold.
50. All smiles ain't happy.
51. All goodbyes ain't gone.
52. All that feels good *to* you ain't good *for* you.

53. Your mind makes as much noise working as a gnat in a boxcar.
54. The early bird catches the worm.
55. Keep all of those strange and different women out of your house.
56. Sweep around your own front door before you sweep around someone else's.
57. You want to get rid of that person living in your house, sweep behind them when they leave.
58. It's a poor rat that don't have but one hole to run into.
59. Don't put all of your eggs in one basket.
60. Don't let your right hand know everything your left hand is doing.
61. Nothing beats a failure but a try.
62. Don't always toot your own horn; if it is good enough, someone else will see it.
63. The best defense is to live well.
64. I don't fatten frogs for snakes.

65. Haste makes waste.
66. If it is worth doing, then it is worth doing well.
67. White people in the North don't care how high you get, just don't get close; white people in the South don't care how close you get, just don't get high.
68. "Niggas" and flies, but most days I will take the flies.
69. Don't let your mouth write checks that your butt can't cash.
70. The only "can't" is a butt head cow can't hook because she doesn't have any horns.
71. Kids will make you shed many a tear.
72. One bird in the hand is worth two birds in the bush.
73. Don't count your chickens until the eggs have hatched.
74. If it walks like a duck, talks like a duck and quacks like a duck, then it must be a duck.
75. If you dance to the music, you will have to pay the piper.
76. Don't invite the devil in; he will never want to leave.

77. I would rather drink muddy water and sleep in a hollow log than tolerate this…
78. Listen to the whispers so you won't have to hear the screams.
79. Man is a child of God by creation, but he is a child of the devil by choice.
80. Don't bite the hand that feeds you.
81. An ounce of prevention is worth a pound of cure.
82. A person is known by the company he keeps
83. Fool me once shame on you; fool me twice, shame on me.
84. You can lead a horse to water but you can't make him drink.
85. Blood never does wash clean.
86. Don't throw good money after bad.
87. I am too old of a cat to be "punked" by a kitten.
88. A man is a father until he takes another wife, but a woman is a mother her whole entire life.

89. Momma's baby, daddy's maybe.
90. If you feed children long enough, they will start to look like you, even if they are not your biological children.
91. Any male can be a daddy, but it takes a man to be a father.
92. Blood is thicker than water.
93. Family doesn't mean you came from the same womb; it means you have been in the battle together.
94. Choose your boyfriend wisely because you are choosing for you and your children.
95. Always have a plan B in case plan A doesn't work.
96. The race doesn't go to the swiftest, but to the one who endures to the end.
97. It's not how you start out but how you finish that makes the difference.
100. Don't despise old age. It is a condition denied to many.
101. Be careful how you treat people. You meet the same faces going up as you do coming down.

102. Sometimes you get the bear and sometimes the bear gets you.
103. Experience is the best teacher.
104. Black folks buy their wants and beg their needs.
105. You must bend the sapling while it is young.
106. Don't let your eyes be bigger than your belly.
107. If you can see the invisible, you can do the impossible
108. Don't build a house where you were meant to pitch a tent
109. What senses do we lack that causes us not to know there is a whole another dimension around us

And when the student is ready, the teacher will come. Our children are out greatest teachers.

Call to Forgiveness – Affirmation
"From today I choose to forgive all hurts, past, present and future. I forgive everyone who has wronged

me and I forgive myself for when I have wronged me. We must forgive as we have been forgiven."

I choose to be free today!

(If you need to be moved by love, and I mean real love, you must first realize that God is love and if you have never accepted God's love, through his son Jesus Christ, I want to offer that to you now).

If you want to receive salvation from your sins and the right to live eternally with Christ today, please repeat the following words.

Sinner's Prayer: "Father, I realize that I am a sinner. I have sinned against an eternal God. I am sorry for my sins. I ask Jesus to come into my life and I will make him Lord and Savior from today forward."

My husband and I in the same hospital and the same hospital room…Healing was taking place!

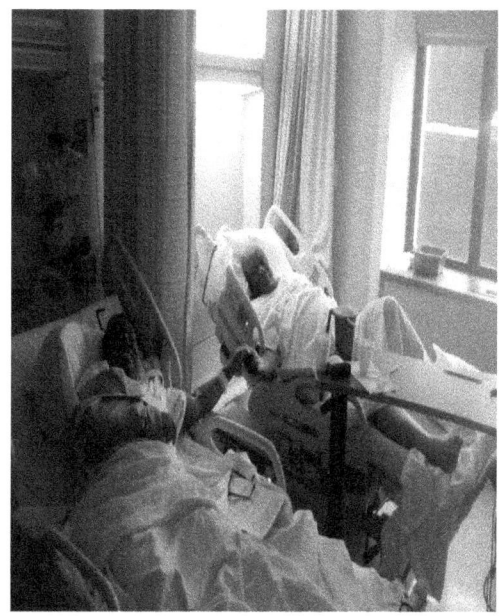

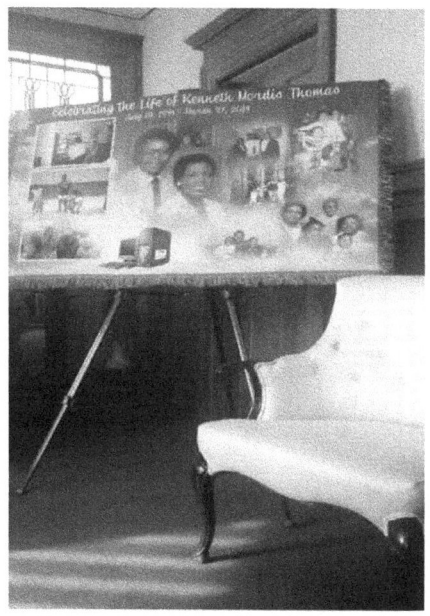

My husband's memorial tapestry at his funeral

The "Port of No Return" in Benin Republic, West Africa.

The "Port of Return" where Mother Africa is welcoming the African Diaspora back home.

www.ingramcontent.com/pod-product-compliance
Lightning Source LLC
Chambersburg PA
CBHW050747100426
42744CB00012BA/1924